LOST
DETROIT

LOST DETROIT

STORIES BEHIND THE MOTOR CITY'S MAJESTIC RUINS

DAN AUSTIN

PHOTOGRAPHY BY SEAN DOERR

Charleston · London

THE
History
PRESS

Published by The History Press
Charleston, SC 29403
www.historypress.net

First published 2010
Second printing 2010
Third printing 2010
Fourth printing 2011
Fifth printing 2011
Sixth printing 2011
Seventh printing 2012
Eighth printing 2013

Manufactured in the United States

ISBN 978.1.59629.940.5

Library of Congress Cataloging-in-Publication Data
Austin, Dan.
Lost Detroit : stories behind the Motor City's majestic ruins / Dan Austin ; photography by Sean Doerr.
p. cm.
ISBN 978-1-59629-940-5
1. Historic buildings--Michigan--Detroit. 2. Historic buildings--Michigan--Detroit--Pictorial works. 3. Abandoned buildings--Michigan-
-Detroit. 4. Abandoned buildings--Michigan--Detroit--Pictorial works. 5. Architecture--Michigan--Detroit. 6. Architecture--Michigan-
-Detroit--Pictorial works. 7. Detroit (Mich.)--Buildings, structures, etc. 8. Detroit (Mich.)--Buildings, structures, etc.--Pictorial works. 9.
Detroit (Mich.)--History. 10. Detroit (Mich.)--History--Pictorial works. I. Doerr, Sean. II. Title.
F574.D48A2 2010
977.4'34--dc22
2010020764

To the city of Detroit:

Speramus Meliora; Resurget Cineribus

CONTENTS

FOREWORD

Architecture critics sometimes get so immersed in the jargon of their trade—entablatures and plinths and the like—that they forget that buildings get built for flesh-and-blood people. In this important book, Dan Austin and Sean Doerr have restored the real people to many of Detroit's architectural landmarks, and not a moment too soon. The "lost" buildings of their title still stand, or rather totter, in a dilapidated state, their histories fading like the paint on their walls. The buildings themselves may not long survive. But thanks to this book and the efforts of Austin and Doerr, the stories of these buildings, and the stories of the people who built them and used them, will endure.

Who were these lost Detroiters? Mayors and matrons, train conductors and auto workers, honeymooners and jitterbugging young couples out for a Saturday night—all the rich panoply of faces that make up Detroit's story. The buildings they inhabit in these pages—the Michigan Central Station, Vanity Ballroom, Cass Tech High School and others—held a central place in the story of Detroit's Auto Century. It was America's story,

too. Detroiters lived, loved, toiled, played, celebrated and dreamed great dreams in these buildings and thereby helped shape a nation.

This book is blunt about the deterioration of these landmarks. But the reader need not fear or expect another of those dreary celebrations of ruins that came into vogue a few years ago. These structures stand today as ghost buildings, to be sure, and some of the photos may make you cry. But more often, the photographs here will have you staring in wonder at the splendor and the plenty of what once was.

So don't worry if you think architecture is beyond you, or if you don't know a frieze from a fresco. Austin and Doerr are good guides, gently leading the uninitiated through many rooms and hallways of Detroit's all-but-forgotten story. It's a fascinating journey, well worth the price of a ticket.

John Gallagher
Detroit Free Press Architecture Critic

BRODERICK TOWER

Thousands of Detroiters once got their teeth drilled high in the sky above the bustling streets of downtown.

The Broderick Tower, one of the city's most recognizable skyscrapers, opened in 1927 as the Eaton Tower, named for what was then one of Detroit's most recognizable families. Theodore H. Eaton came to Detroit in 1838 and invested his savings in a run-down drugstore that had folded in the Panic of 1837. At the time, Detroit was just an out-of-the-way frontier town of about eight thousand, but the twenty-three-year-old Eaton had pioneering in his blood: He was a direct descendant of Thomas Eaton, who helped settle the New World in 1660.

Eaton bought the Riley and Ackerly drugstore, a bet on Detroit that would pay off. He stockpiled paints, soaps and other supplies for the ships that came sailing into Detroit, often staying open late into the night so as to not miss a ship coming in, the *Detroit Free Press* noted in 1953. Eaton adapted his firm to Detroit's changing business climate. As wool mills opened in the city, Eaton started selling them chemicals, dyes and machinery. He taught his son, Theodore H. Eaton Jr., the family trade, and the younger Eaton oversaw the company switch to selling dry cleaning supplies and heavy chemicals for the city's booming auto industry. But it was Berrien C. Eaton, the grandson of the company's founder, who would build a lasting monument to his family's legacy.

BUILDING A BEHEMOTH

Berrien Eaton took over the company in 1920 and also was a trustee of the Eaton estate. His father bought the

Today, the Broderick Tower is a ghostly specter looming over Grand Circus Park. The towering landmark closed in 1985, other than a restaurant space on the ground floor.

Opposite: The Broderick Tower in 1928, shortly after opening as the Eaton Tower. It was brilliantly illuminated at night and could be seen for miles. Advertisements for its office space declared it "a beauty by day—a jewel by night." *Photo from the* Detroit Free Press *archives*.

The crown of the Broderick silently towers 370 feet above downtown Detroit. It is one of the tallest abandoned buildings in the United States.

site of the Broderick on May 25, 1904, then home to the Gladwin Building, a six-story structure built in 1896. The parcel is located on the southeastern corner of Grand Circus Park and Woodward Avenue, the city's main thoroughfare. Before the Gladwin, the land had been home to everything from the Grand Circus Hotel to Turkish baths.

On July 10, 1926, Berrien Eaton announced that the estate would build a thirty-four-story, classically inspired shaft with elaborate Baroque-style ornamentation at the top. The family tapped architect Louis Kamper for the job, and his son Paul L. Kamper served as associate architect. The tab for the building came in at about $1.75 million (about $21.5 million today, when adjusted for inflation). Work started on the 370-foot behemoth of Indiana limestone on September 1, 1926, a building that would be "a landmark worthy of Detroit and the street on which it stands," the *Detroit News* wrote in December 1926.

On March 3, 1927, Berrien Eaton drove the final rivet into the skyscraper bearing his family's name. Paul Kamper handed Eaton the red-hot metal during a ceremony on the thirty-third floor. When it opened about a year after it was announced, it was the second-tallest building in the city, behind the Book Tower. Starting in mid-May 1927, the top of the tower "blazed forth" with powerful floodlights illuminating the top four floors of its crown, the *Free Press* reported at the time. The sight was visible for miles around, and advertisements for its office space declared it "a beauty by day—a jewel by night."

The building was full of marble wainscoting. Its lobby featured Belge marble with a travertine marble floor. The lobby's slender but ornate barreled ceiling led clients to the five elevators that would zip them above the bustling streets below. The elevator doors were made of bronze and featured reliefs of Zeus riding in a chariot wielding fists full of lightning bolts. All of the elevator corridors throughout the building were finished in Botticino marble with floors of Tennessee marble. It had retail stores and shops on the first five floors. The rest was for small businesses and professional offices serving tens of thousands of Detroiters over the years. Lawyers, accountants, a dozen barbershops and dozens more medical offices, made their home there. "At one time, there were so many doctors' offices that it was practically a medical center," the *Free Press* recalled in January 1970. Radio station WJLB also was housed in the tower.

High Times

The prime location and soaring height enabled the building to prosper for decades. On July 1, 1944, the tower was sold for an undisclosed price to a group headed by insurance broker David F. Broderick. Broderick moved his business offices into the building and renamed the Eaton after himself. He also converted the thirty-third floor into a suite where he could entertain his friends and business associates. Broderick died in 1957, and his

In many rooms of the thirty-four-story tower, time has stood still. Here, a dentist chair is one of the reminders of the building's past, the whirr of the drills long since silenced.

Opposite: The lobby's slender but ornate barreled ceiling is still mostly intact and features walls lined with rich marble. Several redevelopment plans proposed in recent years have failed, but its owner plans to try again in July 2010.

The former sky bar at the top of the tower, where David Broderick used to entertain friends and business associates, offers views unmatched downtown.

family sold the building in September 1966. It was sold again in April 1969 to George Fleischer and Bernard Glieberman, but by this point, the building was starting to show its age. Most downtown office buildings still boasted 90 percent occupancy rates at the time, but the Broderick was hovering around 70 percent. They set out to reinvent the building, "and the very first thing we did was raise the rents," Fleischer told the *Free Press* in 1970. They also embarked on a remodeling project, installing drop ceilings, air conditioning and fluorescent lighting. "We bought a slum building in a good area," Fleischer told the *Free Press* in January 1970. "We don't subscribe to the theory that downtown Detroit is dying." But he couldn't have been more wrong.

Businessman Michael Higgins and a group of investors acquired the building in 1976 and have owned it ever since. During the mid-'70s, Higgins had been investing in several major downtown buildings while others were abandoning the city. "You might say in retrospect that he was making the wrong bets and they were making the right ones," said Fred J. Beal, president of JC Beal Construction, which has been working to redevelop the Broderick. That bad bet was because the city continued to bleed commercial tenants—and the Broderick was far from exempt. Most of the tower's doctors had moved their offices to the suburbs. The exodus became like a cancer. The practitioners had all benefitted from the one-stop medical shopping, and once many had left, the rest followed. Tenants complained that heat, water, security and other services were uncertain at best.

In the mid-1980s, as the building was limping along at about the break-even point with 40 to 50 percent vacancy, Higgins was approached by an investor who bought the Broderick on a land contract and wanted to convert the tower from office space into a residential building. The new owner encouraged the remaining office tenants to leave while planning his project, which never came to fruition. The building reverted to the Higgins group under the terms of the land contract, but because the investor had let the tenants leave, the building was now empty save for the first-floor restaurant space. The Broderick has remained vacant since 1985. On October 11, 1991, the Witherell Corp., of which Higgins was vice-president, filed for chapter 11 reorganization, owing $75,000 in unpaid utilities, among other debts. After the bankruptcy, Higgins retained ownership of the building and continued to seek a plan to renovate the Broderick.

In the meantime, artist Robert Wyland, who grew up in nearby Madison Heights, Michigan, painted a 108-foot mural of humpback whales on the Broderick's windowless eastern wall. The piece, titled *Whale Tower*, took three and a half days to complete and was dedicated on October 13, 1997. It became something of a landmark, with five-story whales splashing about among the buildings downtown. Wyland, who has painted dozens of whale murals around the world, called it a gift to the city that was designed to draw attention to the plight of saving humpback whales.

Sunset paints an eerie light in the derelict, vandalized tower. The office floors of the tower have been empty for twenty-five years except for the occasional thrill-seeker.

The rooms at the top of the tower feature fireplaces, heart-stopping views and balconies overlooking the bustling city below. A development plan calls for converting the building into residential units and offices.

A forlorn graphotype machine left behind in the exodus sits where it has for more than two decades. This office machine was used for embossing letters onto thin sheets of metal.

The hallways of the Broderick, once filled with the clicks and clacks of shoes and heels, are eerily quiet—a ghostly reminder of the city's once thriving downtown.

Tower of Decay—and Possibilities

Today, the building sits empty and vandalized, with senseless graffiti dotting the marble along its corridors and plaster walls relieved of their plumbing. On many of the Broderick's thirty-four floors, time has stood still. A dentist chair sits covered in paint chips. Drawers sit full of fake smiles from a dental supply company. Office equipment gathers dust on desks. A post office box sits alone in a corner office. It is one of the tallest abandoned buildings in the country. But compared to many other abandoned landmarks downtown, the Broderick is in surprisingly good shape. Despite its many windows left ajar—making it the world's largest pigeon coop—the Broderick has been better secured than many other empty landmarks and is mostly just cluttered with junk.

In 1995, the Detroit Tigers announced that they would build a new baseball stadium next to the Broderick. Higgins said he planned to dust off the tower and turn it into one hundred lofts and a three-story nightclub and remodel the restaurant space. The plan was the first of at least three attempts to bring back the Broderick, each hitting financial snags.

Despite the setbacks and skeptics, work on reviving the Broderick began in early 2011. After more than twenty-five years, the tower is once again buzzing with life. A ribbon-cutting attended by political luminaries and business leaders was held on April 18, 2011. The $55 million project is to wrap up in September 2012 and is to include a restaurant, lounge and nearly 130 apartments.

The Broderick is a sleeping giant that is finally being reawakened, another sign that Detroit is once again rising from the ashes. In July 2006, John Carlisle wrote on his seminal "DetroitBlog" that the Broderick "is the Cinderella of abandoned buildings—neglected, ignored, seemingly ragged and tarnished, yet underneath it all, more splendid and engaging and brimming with possibilities than the others. For now though, it sits meekly and quietly, waiting to be transformed back into what it really is."

CASS TECHNICAL HIGH SCHOOL

In a city filled with factories pumping out automobiles, Cass Tech was a factory of learning, where students were taught to use their hands as well as their heads.

More than fifty thousand students graduated from it, and hundreds of thousands of others attended class there. Among the distinguished students who wandered the old Cass Tech's halls were singer Diana Ross, rocker Jack White, comedians Lily Tomlin and David Alan Greer, auto executive John DeLorean, jazz musicians Donald Byrd and Earl Kluge and artist Charles Wysocki. Aviator Charles Lindbergh's mother, Evangeline Lindbergh, taught chemistry at Cass from 1922 until 1942.

A SITE RICH WITH EDUCATION HISTORY

The building along the Fisher Freeway and Grand River Avenue traces its roots to February 1907, when the school was founded on the third floor of the old Cass Union School, a three-story brick building built in 1860 on farmland donated by General Lewis Cass. The plot of land, today near downtown, was then a field filled with grazing cows on the outskirts of town. General Cass served as governor, secretary of war, secretary of state and minster to France and was the Democratic Party's presidential candidate in 1848.

Records of the early 1900s show that only 35 percent of high schoolers graduated, and only 10 percent went to college. Benjamin F. Comfort, the principal of Cass Union, suggested that fewer students might drop out if they were given industrial training that they could put to use in the city's growing number of factories. Detroit schools superintendent Wales C. Martindale went to Europe in 1908 and studied its technical schools. Impressed, he decided to establish one in Detroit,

choosing Cass for the experiment and putting Comfort in charge as Cass Tech's first principal. The school opened with nine teachers, including Comfort.

The fledgling school started with modest offerings—mostly commercial and shop courses. The idea was so revolutionary that many Detroiters opposed the idea as a frivolous waste of tax dollars. But the idea was a hit with the kids, and enrollment jumped from 110 in 1907 to 700 by 1909. A new wing was added to the Cass Union School in 1909 to meet the demand, but the old building was destroyed in a fire just a few months later,

on November 16, 1909. The new addition, however, survived, and classes continued. Cass Tech graduated its first class in 1910, though it was only 6 or 7 students. The next year, the council approved $225,000 (more than $5 million today, when adjusted for inflation) to build a new building on the site of Cass Union. The triangular-shaped building was named Cass Technical High School and formally opened on October 23, 1912.

But even with the new quarters, Cass Tech's surging enrollment rendered the building too small by the time it opened. The waiting list for enrollment was limited to

When the school district opened a new Cass Technical High School in 2005, the historic structure was left to rot and had been ravaged by scrappers. Despite a last-minute effort by alumni and preservationists to save it, the historic structure was torn down in the summer of 2011 at a cost of more than $3 million.

Opposite: Cass Tech opened in 1922 on land donated by its namesake, Lewis Cass, a Michigan governor, Democratic presidential candidate, U.S. secretary of state and secretary of war. *Photo from the* Detroit Free Press *archives*.

School's out forever. The desks, blackboards, screen and television sit right where they were when the building closed in 2005. The debt-ridden school district has been criticized for such waste.

two hundred, yet hundreds more applied. The school started offering evening classes to shift class loads. Even then, it was said that it was nearly impossible to move through the halls during class changes.

By 1915, Detroit was building two-thirds of the country's automobiles, and Detroit's population had skyrocketed from 465,766 in 1910 to just shy of 1 million ten years later. The combination of the city's booming industry and booming population was enough to convince the city that a new building was necessary. Construction didn't begin until 1916, but by the time the money was there, there was a war waging. As the government started clamping down on wartime spending, construction was delayed yet again.

WHEN OLD CASS TECH WAS NEW

The Detroit firm Malcolmson & Higginbotham was selected for the job, and the eight-story building finally opened on September 11, 1922. It cost about $3.93 million to build (about $50.9 million today). Mayor James Couzens was outraged, lampooning the project for being poorly planned and over budget, and the city's fire marshal deemed it a fire hazard. But educators praised the building as being as beautiful as it was successful. The High School of Commerce took over the old Cass Tech building, focusing on business education and serving as a finishing school for female students in such areas as secretarial skills, typing, penmanship, shorthand and bookkeeping.

Cass Tech "is by far the largest, most modern and most fully equipped of any high school not only in Detroit but in Michigan as well, and it ranks among the largest in the country," with room for nearly forty-four hundred students and fifty classrooms, the *Detroit News* wrote in September 1922. The construction of Cass Tech was a first in Detroit; not only had a technical school been built, but the city began to shift from a classical concept of education to a practical one designed to prepare students for the job market. The school was essentially a college-prep high school, where the top scholar was more honored than the star quarterback of the football team.

"I went to the University of Michigan my freshman year, and I talked to people who had gone to Cass Tech, and they would talk about having qualitative analysis, quantitative analysis and organic chemistry in high school," said Mike Poterala, who taught college-prep math at Cass Tech from 1965 to 1996. "I've heard a lot of stories about Cass students who went away to college and found college easier than what they had in high school."

The new Cass was connected to the High School of Commerce by the Victory Memorial Arch, a second-floor Gothic-style bridge that crossed High Street (later known as Vernor Highway). It opened on January 31, 1922, and was dedicated to the city's high schoolers who died in World War I. Carved on a center panel in relief

Many of the classrooms look like class just got out. Posters and paintings still cling to the walls, and supplies still fill cabinets.

The district left nearly everything inside when it moved out, from bowling pins to tables and chairs.

were the words: "Victory Memorial, Great World War, 1917–19." It was built to save time when the teachers and pupils changed classes between buildings and to protect them from inclement weather. The concept was designed by Mr. Ray, a Cass Tech English teacher, and made of Indiana limestone. Its cost was $400,000 (about $5.2 million today).

LIKE A FACTORY

The school's exterior is covered in brick and limestone, its vestibules are lined with marble and bas reliefs with industrial motifs flank the entrances. Light courts allow for natural light to pour into the building. The halls have terrazzo floors and originally had barreled ceilings, though they were later covered with drop ceilings.

The first floor was home to a gymnasium with an indoor track along a mezzanine, the teacher's lounge (complete with fireplace) and a three-thousand-seat auditorium that was said to be near acoustically perfect. Floor after floor of the 831,000-square-foot building was packed with pharmacy, chemistry and physics laboratories, machine shops and mechanical drawing classrooms. The seventh floor had a foundry, baking and kitchen classrooms and the school's original lunchroom, which could feed up to one thousand students at a time.

One of the high school's pools is now filled with dust and fallen plaster instead of water and splashing students.

From its humble beginnings with classes in pattern-making and drafting, Cass would grow to offer everything from bacteriology to chemical biology to metallurgy to nuclear physics. As technology changed, so did the school's curricula. When airplanes seemed the limit, Cass added aeronautics. When man aimed to land on the moon, it started offering astronautics. Unlike other schools in the city, where enrollment was dictated by geography, Cass Tech's student body was determined by achievement. Students citywide took an achievement test, and only the best and brightest were admitted to Cass. Because it pulled students from all over the sprawling metropolis, some Cass students had to ride buses ninety minutes to get there, the *News* noted in March 1962. It became "an institution," the paper wrote, that was "virtually unparalleled in American secondary education." By 1942, Cass was not only the biggest school in the city but also the largest in the state, with more than forty-five hundred students.

"Cass Tech has a history of being an engine that drove this city," said Marshall Weingarden, a 1961 science and arts alumnus. "It stands for the highest level of achievement in this city."

NEW CHANGES AT THE OLD SCHOOL

The High School of Commerce, home to the old Cass Tech, was reduced to rubble in August 1964 to make room for the Fisher Freeway. The memorial arch went with it. In 1985, a modern-looking addition designed by Albert Kahn & Associates was finished on the school's west side. The addition added another gymnasium with seats for 750 fans, a lunchroom and a bigger swimming pool—which was mistakenly built using the English, not the metric, system, making the school's "Olympic-size pool" about twelve feet too short. But even with the addition, the original building was falling into disrepair. In 1992, the city's building department deemed the auditorium's balcony unsafe and had it closed. The old pool was closed after the addition was built and left to rot. Only one of its elevators was working in 2000. The roof leaked, and the plumbing often acted up.

In March 2000, the school district announced it would build a new Cass Tech with money from a $1.5 billion bond program. "Replacing such an icon would be a bold statement by the school district about its intentions…to start anew rather than to patch crumbling buildings," the *Free Press* wrote at the time. "Cass would be emotionally difficult to demolish. Generations of Detroit's best and brightest youth have passed stiff entrance examinations to earn the privilege of walking those halls." Ground was broken in 2002 directly north of the old Cass Tech. When the school moved into the new building for the 2005–06 school year, almost everything was left behind, from desks to school supplies to computers to televisions mounted on the walls. Pictures of boyfriends, celebrities and Mickey Mouse still clung to lockers.

One of the three gymnasiums in the high school, this one featuring a running track suspended above the hardwood, which has been buckled by a leaking roof.

The decay of this classroom was accelerated because of metal scavengers stealing the aluminum windows. Many of the building's plaster walls and ceilings were destroyed by the bombardment of rain and snow.

The high school's auditorium could seat two thousand people and was said to have nearly perfect acoustics. The Detroit Symphony Orchestra was among those taking advantage of the design, holding practices there.

Preserving the Past

The Cass Tech Alumni Association had been working to convert the old school into a multiuse center with art galleries, studios, teaching spaces, retail, a performance facility in the auditorium and residential lofts that could take advantage of the pools and three gyms. Meanwhile, the Detroit Public Schools district had not adequately secured the building from vandals and scrappers. Nearly all of its windows had either been stolen or broken, and it had been stripped of valuable metals. A fire broke out in the building's midsection on July 30, 2007, likely started by either vagrants or thieves trying to steal its metal fixings.

"It's gotten more expensive, but the fact is that it was a huge, expensive project to begin with," said Weingarden, who had worked to save the building. "But I don't know what more we can do…We've been doing this for years, and we haven't gotten anywhere."

When you factor in the cost of demolishing such a large building, Weingarden said, "If someone took it off their hands for free it'd be doing them a favor." He estimated it would cost more than $200 million to redevelop the school.

On December 7, 2009, despite the redevelopment offers, the school was listed among fourteen vacant buildings slated for demolition under a $33 million plan unveiled by the school district and funded by bond programs. "Vacant schools across Detroit have been blights on the community and safety hazards for far too long," Robert Bobb, who was appointed by Michigan's governor as the emergency financial manager for the financially and corruption-challenged school district, said in a statement.

Weingarden wrote an open letter in response, saying, "It is hard to believe that sound financial management means investing $5 million to $6 million in demolition when the building can be preserved and repurposed and DPS might realize some value for the property…It is a shame when a civilization destroys important parts of its heritage. Historic Cass Tech was a beacon of education and a symbol of the lifeblood of Detroit, creating a great outpouring of professionals, craftspersons, artists, engineers and civic leaders. When you destroy the lighthouse, ships sink. *Sic transit gloria mundi* ['Thus passes the glory of the world']."

Lost Detroit

Despite the interest in saving the landmark, the school district decided that the offers and proposals were unrealistic and not viable. Instead, the cash-strapped district agreed to spend more than $3 million to tear the building down—enough to buy a ton of school supplies. Demolition equipment showed up in mid-December 2010 and promptly tore a hole in the 1980s addition. On March 23, 2011, crews started hacking away at the addition along Grand River Avenue. Every day, alumni could be seen coming back to pay their respects to their falling alma mater. A mock funeral was held for the school, complete with mourners in black placing red roses on the chain-link fence around the demolition site. The last of mighty Cass Tech came down in early August 2011, leaving behind a large dirt lot along the freeway service drive and one of the city's major thoroughfares.

It is yet another storied piece of Detroit's past, truly lost forever.

EASTOWN THEATRE

Eastown Theatre patrons went from downing popcorn to downing tabs of LSD. The theatre is the last survivor of Detroit's four major neighborhood movie palaces, but its legacy was made as one of the city's most notorious drug-infused rock venues.

With the rise of movies and the city's fortunes in the 1920s, Detroit got a number of palatial movie palaces. And as Detroit continued to sprawl and grow, enterprising theatre owners decided to bring downtown's movie palaces to the neighborhoods. The west side got the Grand Riviera. The southwest got the Hollywood. The north got the Uptown. And the east side got the Eastown.

The Eastown opened on Harper Avenue near Van Dyke at 6:30 p.m. on October 1, 1931, with the movie *Sporting Blood*, starring Clark Gable. Advertisements in newspapers at the time declared the theatre's opening as the "dawn of a new entertainment era" and invited Detroiters to "thrill to the glory of Detroit's newest, finest Palace of Happiness." The ads also proclaimed the theatre's opening as "the most glorious event in the history of east Detroit." Business owners and merchants in the neighborhood took part in the celebration by decorating the surrounding streets for the grand opening.

With twenty-five hundred seats, it was comparable in size and elegance to most of the downtown theatres. The Eastown was built solely for "talking pictures," and when it opened, admission was fifteen cents for afternoons, a quarter for evenings and thirty-five cents for Saturday and Sunday evenings. Children got in any time for a dime. Patrons would get dressed up for a night at the movies, and uniformed ushers would guide them to their seats.

The complex was built for the Publix movie chain, but in 1934 the Eastown was taken over by Wisper &

The Eastown's exterior is covered in reliefs and still grand, though the attached apartment building has suffered fire damage. The building's location in a rough part of town hinders its chances of survival.

Opposite: The Eastown Theatre opened in a neighborhood on the city's east side on October 1, 1931, with *Sporting Blood*, starring Clark Gable. *Photo courtesy of the Walter P. Reuther Library.*

A beam of light peeks through a hole in the roof into the magnificent auditorium of the Eastown. The Eastown offered the extravagance of downtown's movie palaces in a neighborhood setting.

Wetsman, one of the largest independent operators of movie theatres in metro Detroit at the time. It was designed by architect V.J. Waier, who used a blend of classical styles for an interior that was mostly Baroque. The building was constructed between 1926 and 1930 and featured a lit dome in the auditorium and a gold-gilded ceiling. The lobby featured imported marble with a wide, elegant marble stairway flowing into the mezzanine. Like those theatres downtown, the Eastown featured office space and stores, but it also had thirty-five apartments. In addition, it had the grand Eastown Ballroom, with large arched windows, a band shell and an oak dance floor. Up to three hundred people could dine there on fine linen and elegant china or attend weddings and banquets.

FROM MOVIE SHOWS TO ROCK SHOWS

The Eastown spent nearly four decades thrilling Detroiters as a movie house until it closed in 1967. But it was far from dead. Around this time, many old movie houses and ballrooms, like the Grande Ballroom and the Michigan Theatre, were being converted into rock venues. The once opulent movie palace saw its seats ripped out in order to cram more humanity onto the floor, and much of its adornment was removed. It was in this incarnation that the Eastown became one of the foremost places to see rock 'n' roll in town—and one of its most notorious concert halls.

On May 29, 1969, the theatre reopened with its first rock show, with SRC as the headliner. Among those who would play for three to five dollars a ticket were The Who, The Kinks, Yes, Fleetwood Mac, The Faces, Jefferson Airplane, Cream, Captain Beefheart, Steppenwolf, King Crimson, James Gang and J. Geils Band. Among the locals, The MC5, The Stooges, Mitch Ryder and The Detroit Wheels and Bob Seger all took its stage. Ted Nugent and The Amboy Dukes recorded their live album *Survival of the Fittest* at the Eastown, and Joe Cocker began his "Mad Dogs and Englishmen" tour there.

The *Detroit Free Press* quoted rocker Alice Cooper in August 1997 as saying that the Eastown was "the best audience in the world. And I'm not saying that just because you're writing it down. Any other city, people went home from work to put on their Levis and black leather jackets for a concert. In Detroit they came from work like that. The Eastown—those were pure rock 'n' roll times."

While the Grande had a hippie vibe, the Eastown was all blue-collar—and it was rough. "I remember stepping over a body that had overdosed in front of the backstage door on my way in to talk to Alice [Cooper]," Bill Gray recalled in the *Free Press* in 1976. "Decadence was treated casually at the Eastown. I also recall coming back to my car after the show, reaching for an eight-track tape and finding air where the tape deck had been two hours before. That was the Eastown."

That was the Eastown, "a veritable drug supermarket" and major nuisance for then-mayor Roman Gribbs.

A portion of the lobby ceiling still shows original hand-painted details. The Eastown opened showing movies but is best known for its days as a concert venue in the late 1960s and early '70s.

Opposite: This view of the auditorium from the stage shows that much of the Eastown's original grandeur still remains—but it also shows the giant holes in the ceiling and the massive water damage the building has suffered.

A Musical Dope Den

Despite two deaths associated with the Eastown in four months, several drug arrests, twenty violations issued by the Detroit Fire Department and operating without city business licenses for nearly a year, the Eastown kept putting on rock shows. Its capacity was legally 1,727, but some nights it drew crowds of 3,000. In December 1970, Gribbs ordered the Eastown's licenses pulled, but the theatre received court injunctions that kept it alive pending city hearings.

Those hearings weren't helped by the venue's track record. Between September 19, 1969, and December 17, 1971, the theatre received six violations for overcrowding. It also was no secret that the Eastown was a haven for drugs. Detroit police and city officials knew about it, "but fear that any move to stop the drug traffic will provoke a riot" allowed the thriving drug dealing to continue unchecked, the *Free Press* wrote in December 1971.

The final straw came after the *Free Press* launched a month-long investigation in November 1971 into the Eastown. "More than a dozen dope dealers" operated every weekend "with almost no fear of the management, the theater's security force or the Detroit police," the paper wrote that December. Bob Bageris, then twenty-four years old, told the *Free Press* that "the Eastown is not a place for dope. I try to keep dope out." But the *Free Press* investigation found that he didn't do a good job of it. "On three successive nights...

Free Press reporters mingled with the young people patronizing the dealers...watched dozens of sales, and found it a simple matter to buy pills and powder hawked as mescaline, amphetamines, barbiturates, LSD, cocaine and heroin." The newspaper did lab tests and found that some were the real deal and others were phony: "One batch of purported heroin turned out to be an insoluble substance that could kill anyone who injected it."

Angry residents and parents insisted that the city step in, and Gribbs yanked the licenses that month, citing violations of city health and safety codes. A week later, a federal judge declined to overturn Gribbs's order, and the Eastown stayed closed.

The concert hall would briefly reopen under new management for a handful of shows spread out over a couple of months in 1973. Gribbs approved of its reopening at the time but withdrew his support that June following a flurry of protests from neighborhood groups and a survey of residents showing 80 percent opposed the venue reopening. Lizz Haskell, president of a neighborhood improvement association, told the *Detroit News* in May 1973 that Eastown patrons would park in their driveways or on their lawns and "sometimes ran through the streets without any clothes on."

"This community is no place to be staging a rock concert," Haskell told the *News* that July. "This theater is bringing nothing but crime and drugs into our community."

The lobby of the Eastown has been ravaged by the elements and only hints at its past as an opulent neighborhood movie palace. Architect V.J. Waier used a blend of classical styles in the building's interior.

Everywhere you look, intricate details have survived the years of neglect, offering a sliver of hope that one day the Eastown will rise again.

Eastown Productions Inc. carried on without a license but under the belief that it would get one, citing a letter from Gribbs saying that its license was approved. Joe Walsh and REO Speedwagon did the reopening honors on July 19, 1973, before nearly three thousand fans. About fifty protesters picketed as "the sweet, pungent smell of marijuana and popcorn and sweat mixed with the blaring rock music and shouts," the *Free Press* reported at the time. There were several minor shoving incidents between concertgoers and demonstrators, and several people reported their tires slashed. Meanwhile, four youths suffering from drug overdoses were taken to a hospital. The city wound up denying the permits, and the battle returned to the courtroom, where a judge ruled that the Eastown could be shuttered.

New Name, Same Bad Luck

In late 1975 or early 1976, the Eastown was renamed the Showcase Theatre and reopened as a play, music and jazz hall with two thousand seats reinstalled. High school friends Chris Jaszczak, Gary MacDonald and Mike Jeanguenat—all under thirty at the time—were one-time Eastown regulars who loved the theatre but were newcomers to the entertainment business. Jaszczak told the *Free Press* in 1976: "We are the children of white flight from Detroit. Now we are coming back and we all

live in the Showcase neighborhood. We have more than a business interest—we live there."

Ravi Shankar, Tom Waits and Pat Metheny played there during this era, as did the Godfather of Soul, James Brown. Brown brought his sweaty, high-octane stage show for fourteen gigs in six days at the Showcase in December 1976 during his "Body Heat" tour. When Brown allegedly wouldn't pay the Showcase for rent, the venue refused to give him back his $50,000 worth of equipment, and a temporary court order was issued. Brown eventually paid up, Jaszczak noted. After about a year and a half, Jaszczak said he'd had enough and went to work at a different venue. "The gangs in the neighborhood were awful," recalled Jaszczak, now sixty-two and living in downtown Detroit. "When we went out to change the marquee, we'd have to send two people out there or else they'd steal the letters and try to sell them back to us…We'd do a show and patrons would come out and all their tires would be gone."

The owner of the theatre, Forester Hill Management, took out classified ads looking for a theatre company to become a tenant. Charles Reed answered the call, and the Detroit Center for the Performing Arts started staging professional theatre, children's plays, educational plays and free acting workshops. Despite the Eastown's less-than-desirable location, Reed told the *Free Press* in 1985, "I think there's room for good theater everywhere." At its high point, the DCPA entertained thirty thousand people a year with its adult and youth theatres, according to the

The dome of the Eastown's auditorium provides an overview of the beauty that has been laid to waste. The decline of the theatre was accelerated after thieves and vandals broke in, leaving the building wide open to trespass.

Blue seats still filled the auditorium in late 2009, gathering dust and mildew. An attempt to revive the theater for plays didn't last long.

The paint in the long and barreled foyer of the Eastown has peeled, and its plaster has crumbled. Advertisements for the Eastown's opening night in 1931 proclaimed the event "the most glorious event in the history of east Detroit."

The auditorium dome has been largely spared destruction and still shines as brightly as the day it was first painted in 1931.

organization. "To work there was incredible," said actor Daniel Jaroslaw, now sixty and living in Pepin, Wisconsin. "At night, the theatre would speak to you with creaks and groans. It was just so cavernous."

In the mid-'90s, the DCPA planned to spend $2 million to $6 million restoring the plasterwork and updating the ballroom and backstage area and mechanical and electrical systems. But those plans were dependent solely on fundraising, grants and contributions, and "Detroit was really taking a beating in the arts" at the time, Jaroslaw said. The plan included conducting children's theatres, plays, workshops and musicals for low-income youths and renting the theatre out for shows. In return for their lessons, students were to contribute their time, helping out with ushering, selling concessions and cleaning up. But the project foundered, and the Eastown closed again.

THE CURTAIN CLOSES

In the mid- to late 1990s, the Eastown became an infamous site of raves attended by hundreds of people. While in ragged shape, the theatre still clung to much of its past grandeur. Its exotic chandeliers still dangled from the ceiling, and beautiful tapestries still framed the stage. Its electric blue seats were still there, albeit musty and moldy. Then it was taken over by a church group, which housed some of its members in the complex's apartments.

The church tried several times to sell the theatre, starting about 2004, for $2 million.

The building was abandoned and quickly took a turn for the worse. In recent years, a fire gutted the apartments in the complex. Decorative plaster lies in heaps everywhere, though there are still spots where the building's original luster shines. The paint has worn from the proscenium arch in places. Likewise, busts of women on the walls, once beautiful copper and gold, are now plain white, if intact at all. The walls in the auditorium have been washed away because of a faulty roof. The blue paint that had been slapped on the balcony is still there, even though big chunks of the balcony are not, having succumbed to water damage. The chandeliers and railings are missing—as are the moldy seats.

Yet despite the devastation, the dome of the auditorium almost looks brand-new, painted as vividly as the day it was applied—a bright spot that belies a fate that is anything but.

On August 9, 2010, a fire destroyed the apartment building half of the Eastown complex. While the theatre's fire wall protected it from the flames, a demolition order was tacked onto the front of the building. The death sentence means this movie palace will soon join the ever-growing list of Detroit's fallen landmarks.

GRAND ARMY OF THE REPUBLIC BUILDING

W hile its turrets and battlements make it look like some sort of ancient fort built to defend the city from invaders, the Grand Army of the Republic Building's origins are far more humble: It opened in 1900 to serve as a hangout for the city's Civil War veterans.

The Grand Army of the Republic was a nationwide organization organized in 1866, and it had more than 490,000 members by 1890. This made the organization one of the most potent forces in American politics at the time. "There was a time when a GAR badge was necessary for election to any office in the North, from President to village constable," Frank B. Woodford reminisced in a 1949 *Detroit Free Press* column. Such pulling power meant that the group had no problem pressuring the City of Detroit to build it a base of operations, the largest GAR hall in Michigan.

BUILDING DETROIT A CASTLE

The building's cornerstone—marked as a memorial to the soldiers of 1861 to 1865—was laid on July 4, 1899, on land at Grand River and Cass Avenues that had been willed to the city by General Lewis Cass in 1866. Cass is one of the city's most storied and important figures and a one-time governor of the Michigan territory, as well as U.S. secretary of war and was the Democratic Party's presidential candidate in 1848. "Memorial to the Soldiers and Sailors of 1861 to 1865," the GAR's cornerstone reads on one side in a Gothic font. "A.D. 1899," it says on the other.

The triangular-shaped building would open the following year and cost $44,000 (about $1.12 million today). The GAR Building was designed by architect Julius Hess and is one of Detroit's best examples of Romanesque

The GAR, Detroit's boarded-up castle, was closed in the 1980s and has waited for redevelopment ever since.

Opposite: The Grand Army of the Republic Building, seen here in the 1940s, was built as a fraternal hall for the city's Union Civil War veterans. *Photo from the* Detroit Free Press *archives*.

Revival architecture. Hess followed the popular belief at the time that buildings for military organizations should look like castles. The GAR's turrets and battlements were designed to look as strong as the republic the veterans had fought to preserve. Hess's choice of Romanesque details was no doubt inspired by renowned master H.H. Richardson, who produced castlelike buildings with heavy stone blocks, small windows and arches. Hess died during the GAR's construction, and his former partner, Richard E. Raseman, took over.

The city gave the building on a thirty-year, rent-free lease to the GAR. The ground floor of the structure was rented to shopkeepers and a bank, and the north end was open like a market shed and used as such. Fourteen GAR-affiliated organizations shared the building. The rest of it was, more or less, a frat house for the so-called Boys in Blue, complete with an auditorium. For decades after the war, gray-bearded vets congregated inside their castle to play cards and checkers, swap stories and remember their time on the battlefields. In 1930, when the lease expired, the city extended it from year to year. By this point, when the survivors met to play cards in the GAR, it was usually only three or four at a time, and the veterans said they were getting too old and too tired to conduct business.

A New Battle for the Vets

There were only twenty-four Civil War vets in Detroit still alive in 1934. William J. Fraser, life secretary-treasurer of the Fourth Michigan Calvary Association, and his fellow Boys in Blue voted on May 7, 1934, that it was time to give up their beloved home.

"They aren't fit to conduct business, and except for a little sentiment, the old soldiers don't care whether the building is saved or not," Fraser, then eighty-seven, told the *Free Press* at the time.

"We don't make enough to pay for heat and light," Fraser told the *Detroit News* in 1934. "Anyway, we don't need a building anymore, and I'm not fit to conduct business. I can't see very well and can't hear. No one else is any better off. All we ask now is a room where once in a while we can see each other as long as we last. I know that I'll be completely happy when I walk out of here the last time."

Even though the veterans said they didn't care what happened to the building, a petitioning group composed of the local Women's Relief Corps (an auxiliary organization to the GAR), the Ladies of the GAR, the Daughters of the GAR, the Children of the GAR, the Daughters of Union Veterans and the Ladies' National League formed the GAR Memorial Association in an effort to have the building saved as a memorial. Fraser and some of the other men were indifferent to the women's efforts to save the building so long as "they

The GAR's auditorium features a balcony that might have an ugly paint job but is still in remarkable shape considering the building opened in 1900—and has been closed for more than twenty years.

don't use the GAR name," he said. "When the last man of the GAR is dead, the National Encampment wants the name to die."

Other reports of the time had the aging Boys in Blue pitted against the girls in a nasty he-said-she-said battle that played out in the newspapers. Some of the soldiers argued that the women were being selfish and what they really wanted was a clubhouse for themselves. The veterans moved out, and the building was leased to the city's Welfare Department for its Aid to Dependent Children Bureau. The city gave the surviving vets a room and assured them that they would never be denied access as long as they lived. Every vet had a key to the building.

On October 6, 1942, Detroit's last vet, John C. Haines, died at age 100. Haines visited the GAR hall two weeks before his passing, the *Free Press* reported in his obituary. "All my life is contained right here," Haines said of the GAR Building. The city threw a three-day farewell for Haines. There were only sixteen surviving Civil War vets across the country when the eighty-third and final encampment of the GAR was held in 1949 in Indianapolis, and the organization was officially disbanded when Albert Woolson, the last GAR member, died August 2, 1956. He was believed to be 109 years old.

THE CARDS AND CHECKERS RETURN

Meanwhile, the city's Department of Parks and Recreation had taken over the GAR from the Welfare Department in the early 1940s. Shortly thereafter, the building was renamed the GAR Recreation Center, a popular meeting place for groups from Alcoholics Anonymous to dance troupes. The Recreation Department sponsored activities like youth bands, parties for "single persons over forty," theatre rehearsals and card, checkers and chess tournaments for decades. But as a cost-cutting move, Mayor Coleman A. Young closed the center in 1982, citing the lack of residents nearby. The castle was boarded up to stave off deterioration.

Over the years, various proposals have been floated for the building, from a bed-and-breakfast to condos. There was interest from the Knights of Columbus and other groups in buying it. Helping its chances are the fact that it qualifies for historic tax credits for redevelopment, as it was added to the National Register of Historic Places on February 13, 1986. But one of the biggest challenges to redeveloping the GAR has been the Michigan Monumental Buildings Act of 1889, which forbids governments from selling buildings jointly constructed by municipalities and the GAR. The law says the buildings "shall be forever dedicated to the memory of the Union soldiers of the War of the Rebellion." The Law Department contested that the law applied.

The fourth-floor auditorium, where Detroit's Civil War veterans once gathered to play cards and hold meetings, has been hit by taggers and vandals.

THE BATTLE FOR THE GAR

Starting in 1996, the Ilitch family—which owns the Detroit Tigers, Detroit Red Wings, the Fox Theatre and many properties downtown—began courting the property for its entertainment complex to complement Comerica Park, the city's new baseball stadium that had been announced about that time. The plan was to use it as a store for souvenirs or as an entertainment venue. The deal was bogged down for several years before finally dying. In August 2000, the Daughters of Union Veterans of the Civil War and a local chapter of the Sons of Union Veterans of the Civil War filed a claim of ownership with the register of deeds to keep the landmark from being sold.

"We want that building used for its original purpose, as a memorial to the Union veterans and all veterans," Joan Yates, president of the Daughters' local post, told the *Free Press* in 2000. The Daughters drafted a proposal that would have returned a bank to the ground floor and used the building for seminars, banquets, a military museum and balls and parties. The Daughters applied for grants from philanthropic organizations, but the plan didn't come through. The Ilitches backed off, and the GAR continued to sit empty.

On May 12, 2005, the City of Detroit filed a complaint to quiet title, seeking to have the Michigan Monumental Buildings Act annulled and to terminate the Sons and Daughters groups' rights to the building. The suit was settled the following August, clearing the way for the building to be sold and redeveloped. Efforts were ramped up to find a buyer to restore the structure, and a bidding process was submitted for proposals. The asking price was set at $220,000.

"It was built by the veterans and for the veterans and it's a memorial for the veterans, so why shouldn't it be there?" Celestine Hollings of Dearborn Heights, Michigan, said in July 2009. Hollings is the great-granddaughter of Civil War veteran Jacob Allen and became the first African American to be elected national president of the Daughters of Union Veterans in 2002. "There are not a lot of us left," she said of the group. Hollings, who turned ninety in 2010, added: "I've been working on this all this time, and I thought I'd see this happen in my lifetime… But we haven't given up. That's one thing you can be sure of."

When the bids came in that November, there were six contenders. Olympia Development, a subsidiary of the Ilitches' entertainment empire, proposed moving its offices into the building and adding a restaurant on the first floor. Brothers David and Tom Carleton of Mindfield Pictures, a marketing and web design company, proposed making the GAR the headquarters for their new media operation. The brothers had a record of success in the city, having renovated the former Good Housekeeping Building downtown.

The winner of the bidding process was Ilitch, who had continued to buy up most of the real estate near

his Fox Theatre and Comerica Park. The city council, which had to approve the sale, was skeptical of the low selling price. After sitting on the building for a couple of years, the sale to Ilitch was rescinded, and Mindfield reentered negotiations for the building. But those talks appear to have stalled.

The building has been well-secured from the elements and trespassing, and its wooden support structure is in remarkable condition given the neglect it has suffered at the hands of the city. Until the city and a developer can reach an agreement, the GAR continues to sit, having outlived all those it was built to serve.

A tile mosaic, original to the building, stands at the entrance and honors those who fought for the Union in the Civil War.

GRANDE BALLROOM

Its stage was graced by some of the biggest names in music history—and is arguably the birthplace of punk.

The Grande Ballroom achieved immortal status in the annals of music history not only as a rock venue but also for being where the influential bands The MC5 and The Stooges cut their chops.

Designed in 1928 by Charles Agree for dance hall entrepreneur Edward J. Strata and his business partner, Edward J. Davis, the Grande started off as a place to go dance to jazz and big band sounds. Agree chose the Art Deco style with Moorish details, and designed storefronts on the first floor and a ballroom with arches on the second. The dance floor featured springs that gave couples the feeling that they were floating, and it was one of the largest in the city, with room for fifteen hundred people. The ground floor had several retail tenants, such as W.T. Grant Department Stores and a drugstore.

DANCING DAYS

The Grande, on Grand River at Joy Road, was *the* place for young Detroiters to go. Those living on the city's west side hopped on a streetcar or hoofed it to the ballroom's large blade sign, where they'd dance the night away doing the Bunny Hug, the Turkey Trot and the Grizzly Bear. Those on the city's east side headed to its sister, the Vanity Ballroom, which Agree also designed for Strata and Davis (in 1929). The pair of ballrooms, including the cost of land, cost the men about $500,000 ($6.2 million today, when adjusted for inflation).

Through the years, the ballroom featured jazz, ballroom dancing and big bands until the styles lost popularity following World War II. The Grande and other dance halls tried to make up for evolving tastes, offering theme nights like Inter-Parish Nights in the

The Grande Ballroom, seen here with its towering blade sign, opened as a dance hall and finished its life as one of Detroit's most famous rock venues. *Photo from the Burton Historical Collection, Detroit Public Library.*

Today, the Grande sits empty on the city's west side, vacant for nearly forty years and its place in rock history largely unknown by many who pass by it.

early 1940s. But Americans' entertainment habits had changed. Some blamed jukeboxes and records. Others blamed shifts in jazz, like bebop, which turned dancers into listeners.

Mr. and Mrs. John T. Hayes took over running the Grande in 1955 and were determined to keep ballroom dancing alive, hosting live music on Friday and Saturday evenings that catered to seventeen- to thirty-year-olds, many from church and social groups. Fridays were "get acquainted" nights. Saturdays were for dating or married couples and often attracted up to seven hundred couples a night. Men had to wear sport coats and ties.

Mrs. Hayes, who, the *Detroit News* wrote, "reflects the concern of a good housekeeper and home maker anxious to create a wholesome atmosphere for a pleasant activity enjoyed by many," acted as a sort of chaperone and hostess at the Grande, even handling introductions when requested. The couple sought to provide a place for young people to dance the night away in a world that was increasingly embracing rock 'n' roll. Mrs. Hayes told the *News* in 1957 that, even though Elvis Presley was tearing up the charts, the Grande's patrons were "only minorly interested in be-bop and rock 'n' roll music." The dancers did the fox trot, tango, waltz and bolero, as well as the swing and the Charleston, though "the current favorite of our dancers is the cha-cha-cha," she said.

By 1961, the Grande was the only venue in the city with any semblance of what ballroom dancing had been. The ballroom did not serve liquor, "nor do we allow persons who have been drinking on the premises. This is not a pickup place," Mrs. Hayes told the *News*. This "squarish" attitude and the Hayeses' reluctance to change led to the Grande's downfall. It eventually closed and was turned into a roller-skating rink, then a storage facility for mattresses. This set the stage for the man who would immortalize the Grande.

KICKING OUT THE JAMS

Russ Gibb, a social studies teacher at Maples Junior High School in Dearborn, Michigan, was a popular local radio deejay at the time. He took a trip out to San Francisco to visit a friend in early 1966 and went to the storied Fillmore Auditorium, where he saw The Byrds. When he returned to Detroit, he set out to bring The Fillmore to the Motor City, scouting out several locations before settling on the Grande. The ballroom was near where he grew up in the 1940s, and he entered a rent-to-buy deal with the Kleinman family.

"I remember going down there because my cousin would go dancing there, and we'd pick her up from the Grande," said Gibb, who never went dancing there himself. "I was looking and trying to get a deal and had asked other disc jockeys if they wanted to kick in on the place. They were all doing record hops at the time, and they asked where it was. 'You can't do it

Ravaged by vandals and scrappers, the Grande's condition belies its past. "If you went to the Grande Ballroom…you entered a different world," said John Sinclair, a key figure in the venue's rock 'n' roll past.

Previous page: Some of the ballroom's stately details still survive, having overseen ballroom dancing, "Jams" being kicked and decades of neglect.

down there,' they said, 'that's a black neighborhood'… Well, kids always want to go where their parents don't want them to go. And I knew location wouldn't mean diddley if the music was there, they'd come. I knew what I saw in San Francisco would work here."

Gibb would reach out into Detroit's beatnik community and meet people like John Sinclair, a "long hair" who had just done a six-month stint in the Detroit House of Corrections for marijuana possession and was a columnist for the counterculture newspaper the *Fifth Estate*. Sinclair would go on to manage the MC5 and become a counterculture revolutionary. He was the key figure in the hippie collaborative Detroit Artists Workshop, later known as Trans-Love Energies Unlimited.

The Grande opened on the evening of October 7, 1966, to a crowd of about sixty people who turned out to see The Chosen Few and The MC5. Before long, the rock music and the counterculture environment started luring kids from the suburbs eager to shed the ties and ditch the Brylcreem. The Grande became "the embassy for the suburban youth, whose parents had spirited them out of Detroit forever," Sinclair said. "They kind of thought the shopping malls were kind of lame, you know? They wanted to do something more interesting, so they started coming into the city…Just as their parents feared, it rubbed off."

A massive screen hung behind the stage showing light shows and psychedelic water and oil images. The MC5 wound up being the anchor of the Grande, playing there every week at least once. The band's lead singer, Rob Tyner, introduced Gibb to his friend Gary Grimshaw, who would go on to become a legendary graphic artist, doing concert posters and handbills to promote the shows. While Mrs. Hayes had occasionally found herself whispering "to a sweet young thing that her slip is showing," this new incarnation of the Grande would cater to a much different crowd.

"If you went to the Grande Ballroom…you entered a different world," Sinclair said. "It was unlike any of the world that they had presented to you before, and there was no interpretive code, you were just thrust into the middle of it. And if you were lucky, Neal would come with a new batch of acid at ten o'clock on a Friday night and pass it out to the regulars. If you were lucky, you might get one. And by the time you went home—if you went home—you would be in a whole different place mentally, just completely different. So in that way, it was like a gateway into a new and much more interesting and exciting world, which had music at the core of it, and art and images, you know. It was different. It was nothing like Ford Motors, quite frankly."

Gibb had started off booking local acts like the MC5, the Stooges, SRC, the Frost and the Rationals. But in 1967, he started bringing in touring rock acts to play before sweaty crowds in temperatures that sometimes reached one hundred degrees. Among them were Led Zeppelin, John Lee Hooker, The

The stage where the MC5's landmark live album *Kick Out the Jams* was recorded and legends like the Who, the Stooges, Howlin' Wolf, the Yardbirds, Led Zeppelin and Cream once performed.

Yardbirds, Cream, Pink Floyd, Canned Heat, Jeff Beck Group, The Byrds, Big Brother and The Holding Company, Chuck Berry, Howlin' Wolf, The Velvet Underground and the Steve Miller Band.

This shift from local bands to touring acts started innocently enough, Gibb said, when Sinclair brought the band The Fugs in from New York. "Some of the English bands, they'd get on a bus back in those days, start in New York, go to Cleveland, Chicago, St. Louis. So we were a logical stop from Cleveland or Buffalo. It really started as a matter of convenience for the English bands. Once they played the Grande and saw the sound was great, they spread the word. And once word got out in England that there was a great place where the people were cool, and the sound was cool and the city was cool, the Grande became a legend."

THE DAY THE MUSIC DIED

The Grande's final show—and poetically, The MC5's last gig—came on Dec. 31, 1972. Gibb had started booking shows at bigger venues, including the Michigan Palace (formerly the Michigan Theatre), and in other cities across the Midwest. "I had made a lot of dough and was doing shows in other cities by then. It was just part of my musical

A lonely rocking chair sits amid the ruins of a one-time rock palace. The building's future is unknown, but demolition seems almost certain.

73

enterprise," Gibb said. "I could do bigger shows with less hassle elsewhere. The scene was changing, and if you're going to do anything right, you've got to be on the crest of change."

After the venue closed, the building was seldom used, and much like the neighborhood around it, fell into neglect. It was last used as a secondhand store and has been slowly rotting ever since. The roof has long since failed, allowing water to chew large holes into the Grande's dance floor. Broken windows allowed rain and snow to transform its plaster ceilings into concrete-like, uneven mounds on the floor. Souvenir seekers have busted off chunks of the Moorish columns in the ballroom. Vandals have punched through walls and smashed the toilets. Scrappers have looted its plumbing and valuable metals. The storefronts have become a dumping ground. It is an undignified fate for a hallowed site of music history, and its chances of restoration are slim to none. Still, anyone who can squeeze through the gaps in the boarded-up building can take to the stage just like countless legends before them. But instead of roaring applause, the only thing greeting them is the occasional cooing of a pigeon or the wind blowing through an open window.

In July 2006, signs appeared on the exterior of the Grande proclaiming, "Future home of Chapel Hill Ministries." The fate of the building is unknown, but its demolition seems inevitable. When Gibb returned to the Grande about 2008, he said he was overcome with "a wee bit of anger over how a place that meant so much to so many people doesn't mean that much to the powers that be. There's a bit of anger at myself, but mostly at the city that didn't realize what it had."

LEE PLAZA

It went from a towering symbol of wealth to a towering symbol of Detroit's decay. Built for the city's rich and upper middle class, today the Lee Plaza stands ravaged by the city's poor and destitute.

Like the city's Michigan Central Station, it is a gut-wrenching reminder of how far Detroit has fallen from its prosperous past. The Art Deco landmark also is the site of one of the city's most notorious architectural heists.

FIFTH AVENUE COMES TO THE BOULEVARD

Ralph T. Lee made a fortune in real estate in the city, rising from making $1.50 a day at a furniture store to having a fortune worth more than $6 million before the Depression (a whopping $75 million today, when adjusted for inflation). In October 1919, Lee entered the real estate business and started building Detroit apartment houses. In 1940, the *Detroit Free Press* called him "Detroit's most spectacular real estate operator" during the 1920s. By making more than $1 million in ten years ($15.5 million today), the *Detroit News* wrote in February 1927 that "in the building and real estate journals, the rise of Ralph T. Lee is spoken of as 'meteoric.' The adjective is not misused."

By 1935, Lee had built more than thirty hotels and apartment buildings, and hundreds upon hundreds of Detroiters were living in Lee's buildings. "I always know that I should be constantly building more buildings and better buildings," Lee told the *Free Press* in November 1927. And build better he did.

His crowning achievement began in 1927, when he set out to bring a piece of Manhattan to the Motor City. When Lee "made his first trip to New York, he saw many things of wonder—but the thing that stuck

Few buildings in the city have been victimized by thieves and vandals like the Lee Plaza, now a towering, windowless symbol of a once great city's decay.

Opposite: The Lee Plaza was once a luxurious apartment hotel, providing residents with a stately address and a number of amenities. *Photo from the Manning Brothers Historic Photographic Collection.*

in his mind most prominently was the mass of the great apartment houses which line up Fifth avenue," the *Detroit News* reported in April 1927. "He conceived the idea that 'someday' he would like to build and own such an apartment in his home town—Detroit."

On May 1, 1927, ground was broken on the I-shaped, Art Deco masterpiece that would rise above the stately elms of West Grand Boulevard at Lawton Avenue. Lee tapped architect Charles Noble to come up with his seventeen-story modern marvel. The price tag would be $2.5 million—$31 million today. The Lee Plaza opened on December 1, 1927.

A Life of Luxury

The first two floors of the exterior are faced with stone, and the rest is sheathed in orange-glazed brick. The Lee Plaza features Mediterranean flourishes and originally had a French chateau-esque roof of red tile with ornamental lightning rods. The tile was later replaced with a green copper roof. The elaborate ornamentation on the exterior includes large urns, and the walls were dotted with ornate terra-cotta lion heads.

The idea of residential hotels was a popular one at the time, offering "complete home life with all the detailed service of a great hotel," a 1931 brochure for the Lee Plaza said. In the era when real estate and housing were in demand in the city, many Detroiters stayed in standard hotels. In residential hotels, well-off residents could live in luxurious apartments that had many of the features of hotels, such as room service and concierges. The Lee Plaza opened with 220 luxury-class apartments ranging from one to four rooms, either furnished or not. The basement had a beauty parlor, a game room with driving nets for golfers and billiards, a white-walled playroom for children and a meat market and grocer for the tenants so they didn't have to leave Lee Plaza's comfy confines. There also was a circulating library, a flower shop and a cigar stand. In addition, the building boasted an adjacent parking garage with twenty-four-hour valet service.

The Lee Plaza was decked out in extravagance by sculptor Corrado Parducci. The first floor was filled with marble, expensive woods and elaborate plasterwork; its ornamental ceilings would crane necks. Upon entering the magnificent Italian-style lobby, guests were immediately surrounded by jaw-dropping frescoes and Italian marble. Wrought-iron fixtures added more opulence. Continuing on, you would enter Peacock Alley, an eighty-eight-foot corridor leading from the lobby to the back of the building that had a hand-painted, barrel-vaulted ceiling and mirrored walls. Large easy chairs and elegant tables and lamps lined the walls, making the alley a comfortable place to kick back and relax with a book.

The walnut-paneled dining room was said to be among the most elegant in Detroit and could seat 125 people; it also had private rooms for family parties. Across from the dining room was the ballroom, "a stimulating setting for

A look down the Lee Plaza's Peacock Alley, once the centerpiece of the Art Deco masterpiece. Comfy chairs used to line this hallway, where residents could kick back and relax with a book.

life's gayer moments," a Lee Plaza brochure said. There was room for 100 couples to dance the night away under the vaulted ceiling and four crystal chandeliers. At one end of the room was a balcony with a wrought-iron railing that overlooked the room. Orchestras often filled this balcony, where they were out of the way but not out of earshot. Tenants could use the room for balls or parties whenever they liked, and concerts were sometimes held there. It also was used for badminton matches and to show a movie one night a week to residents and their guests.

But with the onset of the Great Depression, the Lee Plaza was plagued by problems almost from the start because of Ralph Lee's lavish spending. The Lee Plaza would help bring down one of Detroit's biggest real estate barons.

Legal Woes and Senioritis

Ralph Lee had sold the hotel to the Detroit Investment Co. shortly after it opened, but by December 1930, the company was delinquent on its payments. The Metropolitan Trust Co. was appointed receiver but quickly went into receivership itself. In 1931, the Equitable Trust Co. took over and appointed Ralph Lee as adviser and building manager. For at least four years, Equitable paid Lee the monthly equivalent of about $7,000 today, let him take food from the hotel's storeroom to his summer home and gave him unlimited room and maid service, nurses for his children and five apartments on the sixteenth floor rent-free. Then, in July 1935, Ralph Lee admitted in court that he, his wife and a third person operated a hardware company for almost the sole purpose of selling supplies to the Lee Plaza and his other buildings at retail prices instead of at wholesale. The following month, Lee was found in contempt, ordered to repay bondholders and kicked out of the Lee Plaza. By fall 1935, the Lee Plaza was bankrupt—and so was its namesake. He died at age forty-nine on March 28, 1940.

The Lee Plaza would be tied up in court battles for nearly a decade, and in the meantime, metro Detroit had been growing—and with it the number of houses. Residential hotels had fallen out of favor, and the uncertainty of the building's fate didn't help retain the clientele. As the building continued to bleed residents, the management started renting rooms to transient guests. The Lee Plaza would continue to barely keep its head above water until it was sold in the 1960s to a turnkey developer, who spruced it up and sold the building to the city in January 1969. The Art Deco giant built for the wealthy would now be used for housing low-income senior citizens.

This final transformation would be the last in the Lee's turbulent life. The City of Detroit put the building in the control of the Housing Commission, and seniors sixty-two years and older started moving in. The Lee Plaza was not the only building the city did this with as it continued to lose residents and the number of empty or financially troubled apartment buildings and hotels grew.

A forlorn piano sits crumpled in a heap on the floor of the Lee Plaza's once stately ballroom, the hub of social life for many of its residents.

The ballroom on the first floor once housed everything from orchestral concerts to movies to badminton games.

The Lee Plaza was added to the National Register of Historic Places on November 5, 1981. When it joined the ranks of the country's architectural treasures, it was noted that "the structure is notable for its excellent state of preservation and it has never been redecorated or remodeled, unlike the majority of the city's luxury hotels." William M. Worden, retired director of historic designation for the City of Detroit, led the effort to get the Lee on the register. "Not much had changed" from the time it opened, he said. "The building was basically intact…The residents wanted it listed and were very proud of it."

Under Siege

Pride alone could not shield the Lee from barren city coffers and hard-hitting budget cutbacks. There wasn't any discussion that Worden can remember between the Housing Commission and other city offices when it was decided that the Lee Plaza would close in 1997. Its entrances and ground-floor windows were barricaded with cinder blocks, but they couldn't keep the scavengers at bay. Once the walls were breached, nothing could spare the landmark from trespass, and from that point on, few buildings in Detroit have been more ravaged than the Lee.

The Lee would become Detroit preservationists' Alamo when more than fifty terra-cotta lion heads adorning its exterior were stolen in late 2000 or early 2001. Outrage mushroomed when six of the lions turned up in the walls of a new development in Chicago. Because the stolen lions were smuggled across state lines, the FBI got involved. The condos' builder said it had no idea that the lion heads were stolen. "As long as there have been graves, there have been grave robbers, and a lot of people consider Detroit a large, unguarded graveyard," Katherine Clarkson, then executive director of Preservation Wayne, told the *Free Press* in February 2002.

In May 2002, twenty-four of the lions and three stone griffins from the Lee Plaza were recovered, a surprising victory as most architectural theft cases go unsolved. But the thefts caused more than $2 million in damage to the building, and what's worse, no one knows where the lion heads are now.

Another devastating blow would come in late 2005, when the Lee's copper roof was stripped, despite it being seventeen stories up and a high school being next door. The building's window frames are also gone, and its interior has been smashed to pieces by vandals and thieves. "Lee Plaza has been reduced to a bricked-up and orphaned ward of the City of Detroit Housing Commission, which has neither the funds nor the initiative to restore the building, leaving it instead to scavengers," the *Metro Times* weekly newspaper wrote in April 2003.

A majority of the plaster rosettes that once filled the Peacock Alley's ceiling have been ripped out by thieves looking to sell them or by thrill-seekers looking for a souvenir.

The grand entrance of the Lee Plaza fronts West Grand Boulevard, once one of the most prestigious addresses in the city and home to Motown Records' Hitsville U.S.A.

Looking east out one of the Lee Plaza's gaping windows toward the landmarks in Detroit's New Center neighborhood. While the views from the windows have not changed much in the last seventy-five years or so, the sights inside the Lee are another story.

DELUSIONS OF RESTORING GRANDEUR?

The Lee Plaza is still under control of the Detroit Housing Commission, which said in December 2008 that it was looking to work with a developer to bring the building back to life. The agency offered to sell the building for one dollar if a deal could be made to work, but so far, no one with the financial means has taken the commission up on its offer. Even staunch preservationists doubt that the Lee Plaza can be saved. Besides the millions that would be required to undo what the city's negligence allowed to happen, the building is located in an undesirable part of the city surrounded by blight and poverty. On top of that, between the roof being swiped, the gaping holes left in its exterior from the stolen lions and every window in the place being ripped out, the Lee could be structurally unsound, adding major, if not project-killing, costs to any restoration effort.

"If the wonderful ground floor public spaces were to be restored, the cost to fix the Lee Plaza could only be justified with very high rents," explained Worden, a dedicated preservationist. "On East Jefferson near Indian Village it might work. On West Grand near Grand River it won't."

METROPOLITAN BUILDING

Once home to the city's jewelers and watchmakers, today the Metropolitan Building sits empty and decaying, an unpolished gem where time has stood still for nearly thirty years.

Between 1910 and 1920, Detroit's population more than doubled—going from 465,766 to 993,678—thanks largely to the rise of the automobile. And with the rise of the automobile came a rise in the city's fortunes. With those fortunes came more places to spend them. By the end of the 1910s, the city was starting to sprawl north up Woodward. Storefronts began to fill the area between Campus Martius and Grand Circus Park.

In 1919, George P. Yost, vice-president of the Central Detroit Realty Co., came up with the idea to centralize multiple facets of a single trade into one building. He wanted to erect a building "at once beautiful, accessible and practical," the *Detroit Free Press* wrote in May 1925.

In early 1924, "an old and unsightly group of buildings" was razed to make way for the Metropolitan, the *Free Press* said. The Detroit architectural firm Weston & Ellington tackled the challenge of building a landmark on an irregularly shaped remnant of land on John R Street between Woodward Avenue and Broadway.

WINDOWS THAT LITERALLY SPARKLED

Excavation for the fifteen-story, Neo-Gothic Metropolitan began on July 5, 1924, and it was ready for business by May 25, 1925. Unlike many buildings downtown, the Metropolitan was not an office building. From the beginning, the Metropolitan was leased to jewelers and related businesses; thus, it often was informally known as the Jewelers Building. Detroiters might bring a treasured

The Metropolitan still stands today, a looming neo-Gothic monument at Farmer and John R Streets. Hope remains that this landmark will be brought back to life, possibly as a residential building.

Opposite: The Metropolitan Building, seen here shortly after opening in 1925, was once home to Detroit's jewelry sellers and repair shops. *Photo from the Library of Congress.*

pocket watch or other family heirloom to the Metropolitan to be fixed. Young men might peruse the counters for an engagement ring for their beloveds. The city's well-to-do would buy pearls, bracelets and other sparkly things.

The first three floors and basement were designed to house retail shops, while the rest was leased to beauty and dress shops, millineries and wholesale jewelry dealers and manufacturers. The fifth through tenth floors were almost all jewelers and were known as the Jewelers Courts. Diamond cutters, goldsmiths, watch repairmen and silver workers all took up quarters there. There was a compressed-air plant in the basement, as well as a refrigerating plant and gas for forges. The eleventh and twelfth floors were given to ad men, commercial artists and insurance and real estate agents. There were 25 to 40 establishments on the first four floors, with about 150 others on the other eight floors.

"If anything indicates the difference between the architectural past and present, that building is it," said John Carlisle, author of the popular "DetroitBlog." "Nobody in their right mind would propose putting a Gothic cathedral in the heart of a downtown nowadays. Yet there it is…It looks like it should house something majestic, something royal or religious."

The Metropolitan was "a modern, fireproof retail and commercial building in the heart of Detroit," the *Free Press* wrote in May 1925. "Aside from being a perfect example of Gothic architecture," the Metropolitan "probably is one of the most unique shopping and merchandising centers ever built in America." A visitor would enter the white marble–floored lobby, "the 'show lobby of Detroit,' and immediately [be] impressed with the air of quiet elegance afforded by the marble walls topped by the heavily beamed, medieval ceiling," the *Free Press* wrote. To the left of the lobby were display windows that "present the appearance of a street of high-class shops by virtue of the variety of fine goods placed therein." Recessed doorways made for exceptional displays and led to several large stores on the ground floor.

"Each floor was a sort of mini mall," said William M. Worden, a retired director of historic designation for the city. "All the jewelry shops displayed their wares, so the windows literally sparkled."

One thing worth noting about the building's construction was how the Walbridge-Aldinger Co. came up with what would now be known as a Double-T structure, in which precast concrete, T-shaped floor slabs are interlocked. The technique, while common today in bridge construction, was rare in the early 1920s but allowed the building to support a tremendous amount of dead weight for all of the jewelers' safes—and makes the building as sound as a tank.

Central Detroit Realty hung onto the building until June 1946, when it was sold to the Provident Mutual Life Insurance Co. It changed hands again in July 1957, when it was sold to three businessmen. But the city's fortunes started to decline dramatically in the 1960s and '70s as the city's residents fled to suburbia, and many of Detroit's

The building's central tower features a large terra cotta knight and shield, helping to accent its neo-Gothic design.

retailers went with them. The rise of shopping and strip malls did the city's commercial business no favors. One by one, Detroit's retailers and mammoth department stores folded. Kern's, Crowley-Milner and Hudson's all folded up shop by 1984. Without such stores drawing shoppers downtown, buildings like the Metropolitan stood little chance of survival. After being sold in May 1977, the City of Detroit took control of the building through court proceedings in November 1978. The city then shuttered it the following year, and the building has sat empty since.

A Gem Goes Unpolished

The usual damage and destruction caused to Detroit's abandoned buildings have befallen the Metropolitan. Metal pipes were stolen from its walls, harvested by scrappers. A deteriorated roof allowed water to infiltrate the building and destroy wood and plaster. Vandals broke windows. It's a story that has played out in countless buildings in the city. But the Metropolitan had an unusual twist. Turn-of-the-century jewelry-making relied on toxic materials, such as radium to illuminate watch dials. And because radium's radioactivity lasts for decades, that made the Metropolitan a fifteen-story tower of nasty.

Several redevelopment plans have been floated since the building closed, but none has gone anywhere, whether because of the economy, the building's location off the main drag or lingering concerns over contamination left over from the Metropolitan's jewelry manufacturing days.

In 1997, the city and state cleaned up the contamination, clearing a major hurdle to any redevelopment of the Metropolitan. The interior retains little of its original luster. Walls have been scraped bare, leaving nothing more than a concrete skeleton on many floors. This is likely due, at least in part, to the contamination cleanup. Still, this makes the Metropolitan a sort of blank canvas for a developer with a dream and a big pocketbook to revive one of the city's most beautiful, though often unheralded, landmarks.

Architect Lucas McGrail, who has worked on redeveloping several downtown office buildings and was on the team that imploded the city's massive Hudson's Department Store in 1998, said the Metropolitan is structurally sound. "Its floors can support a weight that they will never have to support again. It's built extremely sturdy. Cosmetically, on its main façade, it's in fantastic shape. Its rear views are in some peril and need some attention, but I would say to someone who says, 'Well, that's going to cost a lot of money'…that there are more historical tax credits available now than have ever been before."

While the building has been closed since 1979, it remains on the radars of both the city and architectural firms. In January 2010, the Downtown Development Authority started working with the firm McIntosh & Poris to stabilize the Metropolitan's façade and install lights to illuminate its

Looking over the curved railing on the mezzanine to the ground floor below. The building was once filled with hundreds of jewelry display cases that "literally sparkled," said William M. Worden, a retired director of historic designation for the city.

Most of the floors in the building were gutted during a cleanup of hazardous materials left over from its jewelry-making days. Many of the windows have been tagged with graffiti, including these hearts.

Opposite: The wedge-shaped Metropolitan Building as seen from the Broderick Tower. The building's unusual shape was dictated by its construction on what was more or less a remnant of land.

The lobby of the Metropolitan features a wood-beamed ceiling and brightly painted walls. The building has been closed since 1979.

The Metropolitan's neo-Gothic crown is loaded with intricate terra-cotta details that make it one of the most beautiful in the city.

99

magnificent crown and bring the building up to code. That news alone would hint that the building is in no immediate danger of meeting the wrecking ball.

Larry Mongo, a Detroit entrepreneur, has had the development rights on the building since 1988. And while he admits that "I had no plans on hanging onto it this long, trust me," he remains optimistic that the building still has a future. As for more than a decade of waiting, Mongo said it just seemed like "when one thing goes right, something else goes wrong," and he compared some building owners in Detroit to "old gold miners who can't give up on finding gold and just keep hanging on" to their properties hoping for things to turn around. But Mongo is a dedicated Detroiter and vowed that "I'd fight them tooth and nail" if the city ever tried to bring down the Metropolitan. The building will live again, he said. "It's going to happen with me or without me."

Fool's Gold?

While there have been plans looking at making the Metropolitan market-rate housing or condos, any such plan would rely heavily on tax credits and incentives. But getting such credits is never certain. And with the ailing state of Detroit's and Michigan's economies—plus other residential buildings that have come online in recent years—a tough situation isn't made any easier. The current plan appears to be mothballing and stabilizing the Metropolitan until the economy turns around to prevent further damage from befalling it.

"There are a whole host of reasons over the past ten years that nothing has happened with that building," said Eric Larson, president and CEO of the Larson Realty Group, which has been working with Mongo on the building for eleven years. Larson said they're looking at turning the Metropolitan into seventy-five to eighty units of six hundred to twelve hundred square feet each. Despite the building's unusual triangular shape, the "floor plans are workable. It'd be a perfect building, though it has challenges," Larson said, such as the lack of on-site parking. "We've run the numbers as a hotel, market-rate housing, office space, and the only formula that works in today's market is affordable housing. We still think there's a way to make it work, but the city is skeptical of increasing affordable housing while trying to show it's worth more than that."

So the Metropolitan sits, awaiting a turnaround that may or may never come. But one thing is clear, McGrail said. "If Detroit loses the Metropolitan Building, we will lose not only a very unique building, but we are saying we don't care about Detroit's heritage and we don't care about America's heritage, because skyscrapers are as American as mom and apple pie."

MICHIGAN CENTRAL STATION

Nothing symbolizes Detroit's grandiose rise and spectacular fall like Michigan Central Station. And no other building exemplifies just how much the automobile gave to the city of Detroit—and how much it took away.

For seventy-five years, the depot shipped Detroiters off to war, brought them home, took them on vacation and sent them off to visit Grandma. It was Detroit's Ellis Island, where many generations of Detroiters first stepped foot into the city for factory jobs. It was filled with the sounds of hellos and goodbyes, panting locomotives and screeching wheeled steel. But for nearly twenty-five years now, it has been a place for vandals, thrill-seekers, junkies and the homeless. The only sounds to be heard are the hissing of cans of spray paint, the clicks and whirs of camera shutters and the slow drips of water through holes in the roof. Wind whistling through broken windows has replaced the deep-throated whistles of trains.

DESIGNING A DEPOT FIT FOR DETROIT

From 1884 until 1913, the Michigan Central Railroad ran out of a depot downtown at Third and Jefferson. The railroad's business was growing, and the company had started an underwater tunnel in southwest Detroit in 1906. It was decided that another, much larger depot should be built near the entrance to the tunnel, and Michigan Central began buying up land in the city's Corktown neighborhood, just outside of downtown, in the fall of 1908.

By spring 1910, about fifty acres of property for the depot had been acquired with about three hundred small, wooden-frame homes being bought or condemned. It was said to be the largest real estate transaction in the state at the time. Some deals took only five minutes while others took six months. The city forked over morethan $680,000

Detroit's monument to transportation, Michigan Central Station, has towered over the city's Corktown neighborhood since 1913 and cost about $2.5 million to build, the equivalent of $55 million today when adjusted for inflation.

Today, Michigan Central Station is one of the most notorious abandoned landmarks in the country, drawing thousands of curious visitors. To some, it is Detroit's version of Rome's Coliseum; to others, it is a shameful behemoth of blight.

($14.75 million today, when adjusted for inflation) in condemnation proceedings in August 1915, to acquire the property for the depot and the land in front of it for Roosevelt Park, named in honor of President Theodore Roosevelt. The park was part of the City Beautiful movement of the time, which called for grand public buildings at the end of dramatic vistas. Construction on the station began after permits were obtained on May 16, 1910, and the steel framework of the building was in place by December 1912.

Michigan Central Railroad was a subsidiary of the New York Central Railroad, which was owned by rail tycoon William Vanderbilt. For the new station and office building—one fitting of the growing city it served—the railroad turned to the architects Warren & Wetmore of New York and Reed & Stem of St. Paul, Minnesota. The architectural firms had teamed up on the Grand Central Terminal in New York. Charles A. Reed and Allen Stem were known for their designs of railroad stations, while Whitney Warren and Charles D. Wetmore were considered experts in hotel design, which explains the hotel-like appearance of the building's office tower.

The design reflected a return to classicism and romanticized transportation. The station created a majestic setting for passengers, many of whom had come to associate train stations with soot, smoke and noise. And the mammoth proportions of the station were meant to be awe-inspiring and make a statement to travelers about the greatness of the city in which they were arriving and the railroad that was bringing them there.

Michigan Central Station consists of a three-story train depot and an eighteen-story office tower. It is made up of more than eight million bricks, 125,000 cubic feet of stone and seven thousand tons of structural steel—plus another four thousand tons in the sheds. The foundation has twenty thousand cubic yards of concrete. When the building opened, it was the tallest railroad station in the world. The railroad invested a total of $16 million (nearly $332 million today) on the new station, office building, yards and underwater rail tunnel, which was inaugurated on October 16, 1910. The price tag for the station alone was about $2.5 million ($55 million today).

The depot was to be formally dedicated on January 4, 1914, but a fire that started at 2:10 p.m. on December 26, 1913, rendered the old depot unusable and forced the new station to be rushed into service early to avoid a disruption of service. Rushed into service was an understatement. Newspapers reported at the time that within a half hour after officials were certain that the old station was doomed, arrangements were made for trains to start using the new one. At 5:20 p.m., the first train left the new station for Saginaw and Bay City, Michigan; an hour later, the first train arrived, having steamed in from Chicago.

"Before the firemen had uncoupled the hose at the old place, trains were running into and out of the new station," the *Detroit Tribune* marveled at the time. The *Tribune* continued on December 28, 1913, "It was a signal

The impressive Beaux-Arts façade of the depot, with its intricate carvings and columns, is proof of the city's once grand past.

achievement, efficiency of the highest possible standard, and inside of 24 hours after the clock in the old tower tumbled to the ground with the rest of that structure, things were moving as though nothing had happened.

"The new station was aglow, not with fire as was the old one some hours previous, but aglow with thousands of electric lights which glimmered high above the one and two story dwellings. The crunching of frozen pavement, as taxicabs hurried travelers to the new station, and the noise of automobile horns gave the neighborhood an air of commercial growth to which it has been looking forward to for some months past. Moving vans, which had been plying between the new station and the old, and various furniture and fixture establishments helped swell the tide of traffic…The story of the new station's opening on a half hour's notice would hardly be believed.

"Thus the new station stood last night, lights shining from windows high above the building line in the neighborhood, a sentinel of progress and a monument to the old depot which burned, as well as a marker to the railroading of today."

A TEMPLE OF TRANSPORTATION

As one walked into the main waiting room with its marble floors, soaring fifty-four-and-a-half-foot ceilings echoed with the sound of a bustling city on the move. The waiting room was the building's centerpiece and was modeled after the public baths of ancient Rome. Covered by Guastavino tiled vaults divided by broad coffered arches, the waiting room was decorated with marble floors, bronze chandeliers, gargantuan sixty-eight-foot Corinthian columns and three arched twenty-one- by forty-foot windows flanked by smaller windows ornamented with lovely wrought-iron grilles.

Travelers would enter from Roosevelt Park into the building's centerpiece, the main waiting room. Walking through bronze doors with mahogany trim, they'd be surrounded by cream-colored brick, marble finishes and massive soaring arches. There are fourteen marble pillars set against the walls and at the entrance to the concourse. The depot itself, which held the ticketing offices, main waiting room, restaurant and other facilities, was 98 feet tall. The waiting room is 97 feet wide and 230 feet long.

"Everybody knows that Michigan Central Station was magnificent," said William M. Worden, the city's retired director of historic designation. "But for some of us, the first impressions were when we were four feet tall or less…To a ten-year-old, those huge spaces seemed as big as the universe; you got a stiff-neck from being a rubber neck."

Beyond the waiting room, you could buy your ticket from one of the many ornate ticket counters or walk down the twenty-eight-foot-tall arcade to visit a newsstand, drugstore, cigar shop or barbershop. At either end of the waiting room were additional lounge

The depot's main waiting room was modeled after a Roman bath. Its giant, arching ceiling once awed travelers in its majesty and now awes explorers and trespassers in its decay.

areas, including a mahogany-paneled men's smoking room with a coffered ceiling and a women's reading room illuminated by Italian globes.

"It was the most beautiful station in the country outside of New York or Chicago—a feather in the city's cap," Wihla Hutson, whose father was a Michigan Central Railroad conductor, told the *Free Press* in 1982. "You'd have thought you were in Buckingham Palace."

In addition to the arcade and waiting room, the station featured a restaurant with vaulted ceilings, a main concourse with copper skylights and a lunch counter. There also were bathing facilities, where travelers could freshen up or get a shave before getting on the next train, and facilities where they could send telegrams, buy postcards to send home or make telephone calls. At the west end of the waiting room was the restaurant, featuring marble counters and floors of Welsh quarry tile.

The office tower had more than five hundred offices for the railroad's business functions, such as auditors, personnel and other departments. The passenger auditors alone took up the entire seventh floor. Initially, the railroad's various departments filled seven of the floors, making it a "beehive of industry," *the Free Press* wrote in December 1913. The railroad also intended not only to accommodate every rail line running into Detroit but also planned on leasing office space to its competitors, such as the C&O, Toledo & Ironton and the rival Pennsylvania. The tower's halls are lined with white marble wainscoting and terrazzo floors.

"During the '40s, I took many a train ride to New York State, and also to Chicago in the other direction," said Ray Downing, a seventy-three-year-old retired Detroit police officer now living in Henderson, Nevada. "Trains fascinated me as a kid, so each trip was a treasure to me. It seems like we usually arrived at the depot not too far in advance of the departure time. Far different from getting to the airport two hours in advance of flight time now. Maybe there was time to get a magazine from the newsstand, but there was never enough time to grab a bite at the lunch counter in the back. Then it was through the gates and down the ramp that led to the stairs up to the track levels…up the stairs and into the wonderful smell of steam and coal smoke."

At the beginning of World War I, the peak of rail travel in the United States, more than two hundred trains left the station each day, and lines would stretch from the boarding gates back to the main entrance. In the 1940s, more than four thousand passengers a day used to cram the cavernous waiting room and fill its twenty-four hardwood and mahogany-finished benches. More than three thousand people worked in its office tower. Seven days a week, nearly every hour of the day, trains chugged and whistles shrieked at the station. Among those who arrived at the station were Presidents Herbert Hoover, Harry S. Truman and Franklin D. Roosevelt; actor Charlie Chaplin; and inventor Thomas Edison. Henry Ford traveled into the depot from New York riding the Detroiter—and he rode in style in his own private car, The Fairlane.

Looking from the concourse, past the massive columns, toward the main entrance. In the 1940s, more than four thousand passengers a day scurried past here.

Former *Free Press* reporter Bill McGraw first took a train out of the depot in the late 1950s, when he was about six or seven years old. "I can still remember the large waiting room, or hall, and the sturdy-feeling marble, and how vast it felt, and how busy it was, even though I doubt the bustle was as great as it had been in, say, the 1940s. I clearly remember how everyone seemed to be very purposeful; they seemed to know where they were going. I remember a loudspeaker, but I can't say I remember what it was saying."

What that loudspeaker would be saying were the names of distant lands: "Buffalo, Syracuse, Rochester and all points east now boarding" or "Train No. 3 now leaving on Track 10 for Chicago." Everyone would hurry toward the gates and down wide marble ramps toward the billowing, huffing trains with fantastic names like The Twilight Limited, The Mercury, The Motor City Special and The Wolverine.

"It was exciting when the ticket-taker rolled back the iron gates in the center of the rear wall of the concourse and people began to file through," Worden said. "The gates opened to a ramp which led down to a concourse under the tracks with stairs left and right leading up to the platforms."

BEGINNING OF THE END

Passenger trains soon fell into a major decline with competition from government-subsidized highways and intercity airline traffic. Even in the 1950s, rail depots were being abandoned because of the decline in business. In 1956, the New York Central [NYC] system offered the Detroit depot—then known as New York Central Station—and 405 other passenger stations up for sale to cut costs and rid itself of extra depots it did not need. The asking price for Detroit's depot was $5 million, the equivalent of $40 million today. There were no takers, and the depot continued to limp along. Passenger lines were canceled left and right. The massive waiting room was closed on April 1, 1967, and many of its grand walnut benches were sold for a mere $25 each. The flower shop, restaurant and other amenities vanished.

While Michigan Central Station had been seeing about 4,000 passengers a day in 1945, that number had dwindled to about 1,000 by the late '50s; the entire NYC system carried 78 million people in 1945 and only 25 million twenty-two years later. After the waiting room closed, people were confined to the space in front of the gates or in the concourse, and the majestic waiting room was used for storage. The building was hanging on by a thread at that point. In perhaps a sign of things to come, the great clock over the ticket windows stopped in the mid-1960s at one minute to seven.

When the New York Central and Pennsylvania Railroads merged to form Penn Central in 1968, the depot became known as Penn Central Station. But the merged rail company declared bankruptcy only two years later, the largest corporate bankruptcy in U.S. history up until that

The main concourse, where generations of Detroiters once scurried on their way to trains headed around the country. At the beginning of World War I, more than two hundred trains left the station each day.

point. In 1971, the federal government formed Amtrak, which took over the depot that year. The 1973 oil crisis gave train travel a boost, and Amtrak set out on a plan to clean the place up and modernize it. More than $1 million was spent, and alterations to the ticket windows and a new bus terminal were among the changes. A celebration for the formal reopening of the waiting room was held on June 20, 1975—the closest the building ever got to an official dedication. A few months earlier, on April 16, 1975, the station had been added to the National Register of Historic Places. While that move would not save the terminal, it has helped to stave off its demolition.

But all the elbow grease in the world couldn't counteract the deterioration of America's intercity rail system. There were fewer than a dozen trains coming and going each day about this time and fewer than one thousand people working in the depot, running the northern division of the Penn Central Railroad.

"In the '70s, as an adult, I traveled to Chicago by train many times, both for work as a *Free Press* sportswriter and because I had a girlfriend there," McGraw recalled. "The station by then—really only about fifteen years later from my first trip—seemed empty and dark and almost spooky. There were few workers and few trains, but if I recall correctly, there were still a number of signs denoting trains that were no longer running. Nobody had taken them down."

In April 1985, Conrail announced that it would try to sell the station—or abandon it. Amtrak was running six to eight trains a day in and out of the station and said it couldn't manage the upkeep and would seek smaller quarters. It found a buyer in New York–based Kaybee Corp., and coincidentally, the sale was finalized that year on the seventy-second anniversary of the station's opening. The sale price was undisclosed. Amtrak and Conrail remained as tenants in the largely vacant and deteriorating building but were still looking to move because of high utility and maintenance costs. Kaybee landed a new Urban Development Action Grant to convert the station into a $30 million retail and office center. But the $3.25 million in federal money was withdrawn because insufficient progress was made, and the president of the corporation's financial credibility had come under fire when he was sued by creditors.

Take the Last Train to Chicagoville

At 11:30 a.m. on January 5, 1988, train number 353 bound for Chicago became the last to roll out of the venerable depot. It was just over seventy-four years after the first had steamed in. The depot's size and location on the outskirts of downtown, the rise of the automobile and plane travel and the decline in the city's population were all working against the station's survival.

"More than a mere excursion into nostalgia, the shutdown of the Michigan Central Depot should be the occasion of serious reflection about what we once were,

Sandwiched between the waiting room and concourse is the arched retail arcade, once filled with shops and travelers. The station also had bathing facilities, a barbershop, a flower shop and other amenities.

what we have lost—and what, given sufficient will, we could regain," the *Free Press* wrote in a January 1988 editorial.

Mark Longton Jr. bought the terminal in December 1989, and the pistol-packing real estate developer tried his best to keep scavengers out for more than a year, come hell or gunfire. He sought to hit the jackpot by reopening the decaying depot—which by this point had neither electricity nor heat—as a casino. He envisioned a nightclub dubbed The Midnight Express, after the train that had once pulled out of the station, and a hotel carved out of the office tower. But the voters wouldn't agree to add casinos until 1996, and Longton folded before the vote came.

Throughout the 1990s, Detroit's monument to the golden age of railroads remained wide open to trespass and looting. During that time, vandals stole anything of value, such as brass fixtures, copper wiring, decorative railings along balconies and staircases, plaster rosettes from the ceiling and marble from the walls and the bases of columns. Those who didn't steal found other ways to defile it. Nary a window is left intact out of the hundreds that once filled the monstrous building. Inside, graffiti is everywhere, with some tags nearly fifteen feet tall and dozens of feet long. Paintball matches were regularly held inside its corridors, splattering neon greens and electric blues all over the yellow brick.

In 1995, Controlled Terminals Inc. of Detroit acquired the run-down building and erected a razor-wire fence, but the building has been far from impenetrable.

The company is owned by billionaire Manuel "Matty" Moroun, who also owns the Ambassador Bridge and a network of trucking companies. He bought it with the idea that it might hold future value with his rail yard.

Something Old, Hoping for Something New

City building inspectors have recommended that the landmark be demolished since at least 1994, but such threats stopped in March 2001, when Moroun unveiled a grand plan to restore the station as a cutting-edge international trade and customs center. That never happened, and even at the time, some city officials questioned whether Moroun's real purpose was just to stave off demolition. Estimates at the time were that it would cost $110 million to $300 million to restore the station.

On October 3, 2003, Detroit Mayor Kwame Kilpatrick's office announced that he had selected the building to be renovated into the city's new police headquarters. The waiting room was to become a public space with a restaurant and police museum. The building, now nearly one hundred years old, was found to be structurally sound. The project was to have cost $100 million to $150 million and would have taken eighteen months. However, skepticism over the costs, given the city's multimillion-dollar

Giant, imposing columns dominate the waiting room of the depot. Once filled with large wooden benches, today it is filled with only memories and devastation.

budget deficit, and the building's condition and location far from the city's courts and jails doomed it almost from the beginning. The city's auditor general, Joseph Harris, even went so far as to call Kilpatrick's police plan "a fiscal pipe dream" in a memorandum to the Detroit City Council. Hopes that a symbol of the city's fall would become a symbol of its rebirth were dashed.

Since then, Moroun has said that until there is a tenant and a deal lined up to redevelop the property, he will not spend any significant money on preserving it or cleaning it up. For that reason, this once majestic landmark sits as an eerie, debris-strewn monument to Detroit's decline and decay, fifteen years after the billionaire bought the building. In May 2009, he proposed leasing Michigan Central Station to the federal government to redevelop into a possible Homeland Security and Customs and Border Protection headquarters. So far, the government hasn't taken him up on his offer.

"I hate being associated with that," the reclusive Moroun told the *Detroit News* in December 2008, speaking about the depot. "What the hell am I supposed to do with it? I can't sell it, and I won't give it away for a dollar. I can't redevelop it. Who would want to go in there? Nobody. There's no reason. That's throwing money to the wind. Can't tear it down, it's an historic landmark."

On April 7, 2009, the Detroit City Council passed a resolution requesting the emergency demolition of the building at Moroun's expense. Then-Mayor Ken Cockrel Jr. had sought to use $3.6 million in federal economic stimulus money for the plan and then bill Moroun, but the plan was fraught with trouble over the building's position on the National Register of Historic Places and more dire needs in the cash-strapped city. Demolition experts said it would cost $5 million to $10 million to demolish a building of its size and structural integrity.

Today, the monolith still stands, a heartbreaking testament to the grandness of the time before the automobile and the way American life changed after it. In the more than twenty years since it closed, the depot has come to represent all that is the city of Detroit, a towering symbol of decay that cannot be swept under the rug and hidden from visitors. The depot is "the first stop for out-of-town journalists trying to get a whiff of Motown's rusted gears," McGraw wrote in the *Free Press* in November 2009. Detroit's inability to redevelop the depot "reflects its inability to control its image and destiny."

Put simply, if Michigan Central Station cannot be the centerpiece of the city's rebirth, it should not stand solely as a testament to its decline. Conversely, if it were to be restored, it would be making a bold statement about the city's future and the preservation of its past. And it's not like other grand train stations—such as train stations in Kansas City and Nashville—have not been resuscitated from abandoned eyesores into gleaming

The soaring hall once echoed with the sounds of hellos and goodbyes and panting, screeching locomotives. Today, it is eerily quiet save for the occasional gust of wind howling through broken windows.

city treasures. But finding the will and the hundreds of millions of dollars such a resurrection would require are formidable challenges in a city with Detroit's economic and social challenges.

"Demolishing the depot will erase the city's most iconic eyesore, but it won't end the blight on the blocks—no more than pushing the homeless out of downtown will ease the plight of the poor," *Free Press* editorial writer Jeff Gerritt said in April 2009. "Maybe we need this rotting relic to remind us how far we have fallen, and how far we must travel together."

MICHIGAN THEATRE

Generations of Detroiters used to park their seats under the jaw-dropping ornate plasterwork and opulence of a downtown movie palace. Today, they park their cars there.

The 4,038-seat Michigan Theatre was designed in 1925 with an exterior with Renaissance details and a vast theatre, which, like most movie houses of the time, derived mostly from the Baroque. It was simply unrivaled for elegance in Detroit at the time. The Michigan was built on Bagley near Cass Avenue at a cost of more than $3.5 million ($42.4 million today, when adjusted for inflation) and was the only Detroit theatre designed by renowned architects Cornelius W. and George L. Rapp. The theatre was the Rapp brothers' third largest, and it—and the thirteen-story Michigan Building office tower to which it is connected—opened in 1926.

THE MAJESTIC MICHIGAN

In March 1925, wreckers descended on the site and began making way for the Michigan, razing the St. Denis Hotel, a gas station, a blacksmith shop and a Detroit Creamery Co. warehouse, among other buildings. The Michigan complex was the first piece in an ambitious program planned for Bagley Avenue, the other two key pieces being the United Artists Theatre and the twenty-two-story Detroit-Leland Hotel. Before the Michigan Theatre rose in 1926, the eastern end of Bagley was "a wide, unkempt thoroughfare with nondescript buildings lining most of its length," the *Detroit Free Press* wrote in January 1928. "The growth of business on that part of Bagley avenue that has been touched by the magic of enterprise…is one of Detroit's commercial marvels…The average native Detroiter

Movie patrons and concertgoers once filed through the theatre's main entrance. Today, automobiles file in through rolling gates.

Opposite: The mighty Michigan Theatre's giant blade sign once illuminated Bagley Avenue, letting those in Grand Circus Park know where the action was. In the background is the Detroit-Leland Hotel, which was a piece of a major effort to build up Bagley Avenue along with the Michigan and United Artists Theatres. *Photo from the* Detroit Free Press *archives*.

believes that it is quite natural for unusual things to be the usual in Detroit, but this great investment in such an undeveloped district made him wonder."

The Michigan Theatre was run by the Balaban & Katz group of Chicago in affiliation with Detroit's first theatre tycoon, John H. Kunsky. It was Kunsky's flagship in his empire of theatres and opened on August 23, 1926, with the film *You Never Know Women* with Florence Vidor and Lowell Sherman.

"It is not merely a theatre for Detroit," Kunsky told the *Detroiter* in August 1926. "It is a theatre for the whole world. It is designed to be the great showplace of the middle west." The *Free Press* review of the theatre's opening showed that Kunsky was a man of his word. "It is beyond the dreams of loveliness; entering, you pass into another world. Your spirit rises and soars along the climbing pillars and mirrored walls that ascend five stories to the dome of the great lobby. It becomes gay and light under the warm coloring that plays across the heavily carved and ornamental walls as myriads of unseen lights steal out from mysteriously hidden coves to illume the interior with romantic sundown colors."

R.J. McLaughlin's review in the *Detroit Daily News* described the theatre as "a new jewel to Detroit…bound to have its historic value in the city, for another such theatre is not likely to be built while the memory of this is yet green." Ella H. McCormick wrote in the *Free Press* that the Michigan is "heralded as the world's finest… No one will dispute these assertions after having seen this magnificent building, with its opulence in decorative art…its thousand and one features planned for the complete enjoyment of patrons."

The theatre was loaded with extravagant details, from its auditorium to its four-story, one-thousand-square-foot, mirror-paneled, black-and-white-checkered-floor lobby. The lobby was complete with columns and red velvet hangings, marble archways, lavish towering columns, baskets of flowers and large crystal chandeliers. A lovely wide staircase with carved balustrades and covered in lush red carpet stood at the other end. A grand piano entertained guests waiting for the movie to start. Between every pair of columns was an oil painting. All of the sculptures, busts, carved furnishings, paintings and onyx pedestals filling the Michigan's lobby made it seem as much a museum as a movie theatre.

The mezzanine level was initially reserved for black-tie invited guests and had gilded foyers and subdued lighting and was decorated with paintings. There were luxurious lounges, "cosmetic rooms" for women and "retiring rooms" for men. A large replica of a fifth-century Roman sculpture depicting a horse and chariot stood there. It was said that ushers often had to shoo children who climbed into the "driver's seat." This horse and chariot sculpture, a replica of one at the Vatican, is believed to have been the largest sculpture in any U.S. movie palace. Another large sculpture, Cupid and Psyche, was a replica of a work by eighteenth-century artist Antonio Canova.

The palatial lobby of the Michigan helps to explain the term "movie palace." The theatre's opulence was unsurpassed in the city when it opened in 1926. *Photo from the* Detroit Free Press *archives.*

The huge auditorium featured six aisles of seats on each level, side boxes, ten-foot crystal chandeliers dangling eight floors above the seats below, a stage with an orchestra pit and a five-manual Wurlitzer organ that could be raised to the stage. Because films were silent until 1928, conductor Eduard Werner's Michigan Symphony Orchestra and the twenty-five-hundred-pipe, $50,000 Wurlitzer would set the mood for movies. At the time the theatre opened, the *Free Press* wrote that the Michigan's stage was so large that it "could house a circus." Indeed, the article continued, the stage could "accommodate the most colossal stage production likely to ever be required." While that may have been 1920s hyperbole, one opening night beholder still described the theatre as "a castle of dreams and an ocean of seats," the *Detroit News Magazine* wrote in September 1968.

The theatre opened with five shows daily, usually consisting of a concert by the orchestra, two twenty-minute stage shows, singers and dancers and then a film. "And with a policy of any seat in the theatre for the same price, and prices ranging from thirty-five cents to seventy-five cents according to the time of day…it is expected that the theatre will be filled to capacity constantly," the *Detroiter* wrote in August 1926. Stars like the Marx Brothers, Frank Sinatra, Jack Benny, Louis Armstrong, Red Skelton, Glenn Miller, Artie Shaw, Benny Goodman, Doris Day, the Dorsey Brothers and Bette Davis all appeared on the Michigan's stage. But by the late 1940s, changing times led the Michigan to focus mostly on movies.

One of the more memorable stories involving the Michigan and its stars involved Bob Hope. On one of Hope's early visits to the theatre, he said he thought he was headlining. He said he walked around to the front of the theatre and found himself second-billed on the marquee to an actor named Joe Mendi. That might not have been a huge shock at the time considering Mendi was one of the best-known entertainers in Detroit, only Mendi was a chimpanzee that performed at the Detroit Zoological Park. The chimp's death in September 1934 was big news, trumping even a deadly cruise ship fire that killed more than 130 people.

The Curtain's Rise and Fall

After Kunsky's chains of theatres failed during the Depression, the Michigan became part of the United Detroit Theatres, where it spent most of its theatre life. United Detroit had twenty-five theatres in the city in the days before government monopoly-busters forced the chain to divest itself of some of its theatres. The theatre continued to be a big draw under the new ownership, especially among the younger crowd. "The Michigan Theatre had a wonderful balcony for necking with girlfriends," noted Marshall Weingarden, who frequented the movie palace in the 1960s.

While United Detroit hung onto its gem, it would not keep its gem completely intact. With sound fully established in

The grand lobby of the Michigan as seen from what was once a foyer. At the end of the marble-columned lobby once stood a gorgeous marble staircase.

The lobby ceiling retains its intricate plaster detail, though its massive chandeliers are long since gone.

theatres, the orchestra was expendable, as was the Wurlitzer, one of only three five-manual organs the company built. In 1955, the mighty Wurlitzer was sold to Fred Hermes of Racine, Wisconsin, who installed it at his home the following year. Today, the organ still resides there, where performances are given in Hermes's Basement Bijou, a two-story addition done up like an old movie palace.

The Michigan's large, vertical blade sign was condemned by the city and removed in 1952; it was replaced with a less exciting standard sign. To keep up with the times, a wide screen was installed in 1954, which damaged the proscenium arch. In 1953, the Michigan was one of only twelve theatres in the country showing 3D movies such as *House of Wax* with Vincent Price.

With the rise of television and suburban theatres, attendance at Detroit's downtown movie houses had dropped off dramatically by the 1960s. One by one, the grand movie houses' marquees went dark: the Annex in 1949, the Oriental the year after, the Majestic the year after that and the Hollywood in 1958. And that's not taking into account the dozens upon dozens of small neighborhood theatres that closed up shop. Many of those that weren't closed were relegated to subpar flicks, second-run status or worse, porn.

The Show's Over

By the mid-1960s, the Michigan was among the movie houses that had become unprofitable. United Detroit Theatres sold the theatre and office tower on March 1, 1967, for $1.5 million (about $9.7 million today). But the new owners cared only about the Michigan Building and had little interest in running a movie house. The theatre would close four days later, on March 5, 1967, after a double billing of *The Spy with a Cold Nose* with Laurence Harvey and *A Thousand Clowns* with Jason Robard. "There was nothing spectacular about the final curtain call for the forty-year-old downtown theatre," the *Free Press* wrote the next morning. "The last scene flashed on the big screen…the house lights brightened…the audience shuffled across the rich red carpet…and that was that."

Only four hundred people took in the show, a far cry from the theatre's glory days, when its four thousand seats often weren't enough. "I remember when people used to wait in line four hours just to get in the show," projectionist Charles Milles, then seventy-three, told the *Free Press* that night. "In those days we even had performers in the lobby to entertain the customers before they sat down."

The theatre was set up for a date with the wrecking ball, but Nicholas George, a man who operated nearly a dozen theatres in metro Detroit, stepped in to save it in 1967. George, an intuitive showman, bought the theatre and did what no one else dared: attempted to revive it. George spruced up the Michigan, repairing, repainting, recarpeting, re-draping and re-lamping the place. He told the *Detroit News* in 1968 that he had paid more for renting the film that he reopened the Michigan with—

Much of the auditorium's ceiling is still intact, despite being exposed to the elements and car exhaust for decades.

Opposite: The grand mirrored window at the main entrance once housed a large chandelier. While the theatre itself was gutted for a parking garage, this area remains in remarkable shape and still cranes the necks of those who see it.

Valley of the Dolls—than he had for the theatre itself. "The first time I saw the Michigan Theatre, it was as beautiful as any palace I had ever seen," George told the *Detroit News Magazine* in a September 1968 story.

Owning it was a dream come true, he said. But the touch-ups couldn't keep the majestic Michigan afloat, and it briefly closed three years later, at 12:13 a.m. on December 3, 1970. It went out with bells on.

"The last day was something special," Bob Warsham wrote in a letter published in a Theatre Historical Society of America book on the Michigan. "All the lights and coves were lit. Several areas were lit that in three years of bi-weekly movie going I had never seen before. The original paint job is still in the upper areas of the auditorium and is in rose, creme and old gold and despite the fact that it is slightly soiled, it still looked impressive. The loge and mainfloor areas are repainted tastefully and the 'diamond' horseshoe of the loge was all lit in royal blue."

The Michigan's glory had passed, though it would reopen its doors the following month and stayed in business until June 1971. Then the screen went dark for good.

Dinner and a Movie—Minus the Movie

Sam Hadous took out a sixteen-year lease on the theatre with the owners of the Michigan Building and set out on a $500,000 renovation to transform the movie palace into a giant supper club. "I'm not a rich man," Hadous told the *News* in January 1972. "I can't afford to have any doubts at all about the location. The suburbs may now have all the [first-run] movie houses, but I'm going to have something that nobody else has in the state—a fifteen hundred seat club offering the biggest name talent available."

On January 19, 1972, workers started removing seats to make way for the table and chair setup. A kitchen was added, and the inclined floors were leveled into four flat sections, each elevated above the other. The mezzanine was restored, but the balcony remained closed. The supper club opened on March 27 with a performance by Duke Ellington and with a new name, the Michigan Palace. Ellington, incidentally, had performed at the Michigan Theatre back in 1934.

The club floundered, lasting only a few months, and the Michigan fell into the hands of rock promoter Steven Glantz, who turned it into a concert venue in 1973 but kept the Michigan Palace name. Many of the top rock acts of the 1970s performed there, including David Bowie, The Stooges, The New York Dolls, Aerosmith, Bob Seger, Rush, Iron Butterfly, Blue Oyster Cult and Badfinger. But its time as a rock venue would hint at the destruction that was to come. While rock and rolling all night (and partying every day) to Kiss or T. Rex, concertgoers left their mark on the Michigan. Marble met marker. Glamorous chairs and tables met gum. Polished brass and glass

Cherubs still flank the Michigan's massive proscenium arch, just as they have since the theatre opened on August 23, 1926.

met grime. Mirrors met fists. The rock days were "the kiss of death" for the Michigan, said theatre historian John Lauter.

Bret Eddy described the devastation in a letter published in the Theatre Historical Society's book on the Michigan: "We mounted the grand stairway with its red carpet littered with mashed paper cups and some of their contents to the once elegant mezzanine, where we found vodka bottles and beer cans piled in corners…My mind, rebelling at the sordid scenes we had witnessed, thought of ancient Rome having reached new heights of architectural beauty, only to be invaded and ravaged by barbarian tribes."

The Michigan Palace didn't fare well as a nightclub either, and it closed in 1976 following a dispute between the building's owners, Bagley Associates Limited, and Glantz over $175,000 in damage to the interior.

PARKING IN A PALACE

Tenants in the adjoining office building, including the Charge Card Association, needed secure parking and were threatening to leave for another office building if something was not done. The theatre, now in tremendous disrepair

A car enjoys the comfy confines of the world's only Baroque parking garage. Here you can see what's left of the Michigan's balcony and hallways, which were destroyed to accommodate the switch from movie palace to parking palace.

Opposite: The ceiling's detailed plasterwork still survives, despite now looking down on silver cars instead of the silver screen.

and silent, was considered a waste of space, and its owners looked at razing the theatre for parking.

"According to Palace employees, the rowdy rockers sounded the death knell for the Michigan," the *Free Press* wrote in July 1976. "Vandalism and damage to the structure are so great that it is more feasible to demolish it than to attempt a reconstruction. Inside the theatre, mirrors have been smashed, fixtures ripped from the walls, seats torn from the floor and graffiti scrawled on the walls and floors. Most surfaces are covered with mold and soot. Holes in the roof drip water onto the debris-covered floor." An unnamed worker told the paper that "when it's all said and done, it just makes a hell of a lot more sense to tear it down than to try to fix it up again."

But architectural studies showed that literally bringing the house down would jeopardize the soundness of the adjoining office building. The solution was one of the most unusual, albeit creative, fates to ever befall such a landmark: It would be carved into the state's only Baroque parking garage. Cherubs that had once flanked stars of the stage and screen would now flank cars. In 1977, the building's owners paid $525,000 to gut the theatre and build a three-level, 160-space parking deck inside it. The mezzanine and balcony were brought down, as was the grand staircase and one wall of the grand lobby. While walls were knocked out and beauty ravaged, much of the theatre survives today. Its ticket booth, four-story lobby, proscenium arch and part of the balcony partially remain. "We wanted to leave some of the theatre's beauty intact," Leo Cooney, president of the Charge Card Association, told the *Free Press* in September 1978, explaining the decision. Today, the sight of cars parked under grimy, though still gorgeous, plaster details draws tourists, photographers and gawkers in disbelief.

In a twist that is as sad as it is ironic, the theatre was built on the site of the small garage where Henry Ford built his first automobile, the quadricycle. (The garage was disassembled by the auto baron and taken to his vast outdoor museum in Dearborn, Michigan.) The site of the automobile's birthplace was replaced by a movie theatre and reclaimed by the automobile—truly a story that could happen only in Detroit.

UNITED ARTISTS THEATRE

The United Artists Theatre was one of several in Detroit that helped define the term "movie palace." It thrilled hundreds of thousands of Detroiters with its movies and interiors, wowed listeners as a recording studio for the Detroit Symphony Orchestra and developed a peculiar habit of crushing Oldsmobiles.

By the time legendary theatre architect C. Howard Crane sat down to sketch out Detroit's UA, the United States was already enamored with motion pictures. In the 1920s, the area around Grand Circus Park was becoming lined with dazzling places to see shows, each theatre trying to outdo its rivals in opulence and flair. The intricate designs and lavish interiors of these so-called movie palaces allowed working-class Detroiters to enjoy the splendors of the rich. The theatres became as much of a draw as the films themselves and were part of the show. And Detroit's United Artists was no exception.

Crane designed the theatre in the Spanish Gothic style and the adjoining office building in Art Deco in 1927. The office building opened on January 28, 1928, and the theatre followed a few days later. The eighteen-story, 200,000-square-foot office tower originally housed furriers, tailors, beauty salons and even travel agents. The Peoples' State Bank occupied the corner at Bagley and Clifford Street. The price tag on the building was about $5 million (about $63 million today, when adjusted for inflation), and it was the third piece in an ambitious building program planned for Bagley Avenue. The other two key pieces were the Michigan Theatre and the Detroit-Leland Hotel.

Today, the United Artists Building sits awaiting an uncertain future. While there is reason to hope that the office tower can be redeveloped, the future of the theater itself is grim.

Opposite: The United Artists Theatre is housed behind this eighteen-story office tower near Grand Circus Park. The office portion opened January 28, 1928, and the theatre followed a few days later. *Photo from the* Detroit Free Press *archives*.

PREMIER
DEVELOPMENT
OPPORTUNITY

5 Acres

Historic
Grand Circus
Park Frontage

313-983-6200

OLYMPIA
DEVELOPMENT

PREMIER
DEVELOPMENT
OPPORTUNITY

5 Acres

Historic
Grand Circus
Park Frontage

313-983-6200

OLYMPIA
DEVELOPMENT

THREE OF A KIND

The UA was the baby of Detroit's movie palaces, as it was the smallest of the giants. The UA was built exclusively for films—a rarity at the time—and showed mostly United Artists pictures. That movie studio was founded in 1919 by actors Charlie Chaplin, Mary Pickford and Douglas Fairbanks and director D.W. Griffith—then four of the biggest names in showbiz. Detroit's UA was one of three that Crane designed in the Spanish Gothic style for the United Artists Theatre Circuit, following theatres in Chicago and Los Angeles.

The Detroit movie house was considered the sister of the Los Angeles showplace. Crane, who had done mostly classical theatre designs up until this point, was asked to use an exotic Gothic style because Pickford loved the look of European castles, according to the Los Angeles Theatres website. An eight-story, jaw-dropping blade sign clung to the eastern side of the building spelling the name "United Artists" in eighty feet of multicolor bulbs. The marquee was seven and a half feet wide and featured a sunburst design at its base. The theatre's price tag was about $1.2 million (about $15 million today).

The United Artists' auditorium was like a cathedral and was said to be acoustically perfect; it was decorated with Gothic-inspired ornamental plaster and brass light fixtures. For this UA theatre, Crane had colored lights filtering down from perforations in the domed ceiling of the auditorium, allowing for the intricate details to be bathed in beautiful illumination.

The 2,070-seat Detroit theatre opened on February 3, 1928, with the showing of *Sadie Thompson*. The film's star, Gloria Swanson, addressed the audience by telephone, pulling the switch by remote and opening the curtain on the theatre's eighteen- by twenty-two-foot screen for the first time. Patrons paid thirty-five cents for matinees and sixty-five cents for evening shows. Smokers were charged an extra dime to sit in the loge level, which was decked out in silk draperies, tapestries and ornate plaster and light fixtures.

Even though the United Artists was built exclusively for films, this "Shrine to the Motion Picture" also had an orchestra led by Hugo Riesenfield that provided the soundtracks to silent movies during the early years. The theatre was built with a three-manual, fifteen-rank Wurlitzer organ.

Sometimes the United Artists featured reserved seating, such as when it held the Detroit premiere of *Gone With the Wind* in 1940 (the movie co-premiered at the Wilson Theatre, now Music Hall). Among the United Artists' long list of blockbuster premiers were *Hell's Angels*, *Cleopatra*, *Snow White*, *The Wizard of Oz*, *Pinocchio*, *Anatomy of a Murder*, *South Pacific* and *Around the World in 80 Days*. The fact that it was smaller allowed for a more intimate experience than could be offered at the larger theatres. In fact, it was sometimes known as the "jewel box" of Detroit's first-run theatres.

UNITED ARTISTS BUILDING
Job No. 220
No. 53   Date 2-23-28
C. HOWARD CRANE, ARCHITECT
WALBRIDGE ALDINGER COMPAN
GENERAL CONTRACTORS

This is how the lobby appeared shortly after the theater opened. Detroit's UA was one of three that architect C. Howard Crane designed in the Spanish Gothic style for the United Artists Theatre Circuit. *Photo courtesy of Lucas McGrail.*

The lobby has been allowed to decay beyond the point of recognition. Only a surviving section of ornate plaster here or there lets you know where you are.

In addition to premieres, the United Artists was the second theatre in Detroit to install CinemaScope in 1953 and the first with seventy-millimeter films in 1956 (with *Oklahoma!* on February 20, 1956). On July 31, 1957, the Bagley Building Corp. sold the United Artists Building for $3.2 million (about $24 million today) to the Detroit Automobile Inter-Insurance Exchange of the Automobile Club of Michigan for office space.

PORN, BARGAIN HUNTING AND FALLING BRICKS

By 1969, the city had bled residents and businesses following the 1967 riot, and the United Artists' business had dropped dramatically. Without the money for top first-run movies, the theatre switched to showing porn flicks in 1969. Following a brief period of closures, the venue reopened in 1971 as a grind house, showing gore and horror movies. But that operation wouldn't last long, and the theatre closed on September 14, 1971. In 1974, the American Automobile Club moved to Dearborn, Michigan, leaving the office tower and theatre vacant and helping to greatly accelerate the demise of the Grand Circus business district. With no one to watch over the building, it would start to fall into disrepair.

On February 15, 1975, the Automobile Club, which still owned the United Artists Building, auctioned off all of the theatre's furnishings, fixtures and artwork through the DuMouchelle Art Galleries in downtown Detroit. The décor from the theatre's lobbies, hallways, lounges and stairways was sold off piecemeal. Cabinets, marble-topped tables and statues of gods, nymphs and satyrs, as well as hand-carved chairs and benches, all went under the gavel before an estimated crowd of four hundred bidders. Chairs and sofas went for $125 and up; some of the art pieces fetched $1,000 to $2,000 each. "When the last chair was auctioned off, many of the crowd trooped over to the old theatre on Bagley, where a dozen chandeliers, including the ornate 15-foot high pair over the main body of the theatre, were sold," the *Detroit News* reported the next day. At this point, the opulent complex was used mostly as a glorified warehouse.

Starting in 1979, the Detroit Symphony Orchestra used the United Artists as a recording studio for a series of albums on London Records, but by 1983, the DSO said it couldn't continue given the lack of heat and electricity and rain falling through the ceiling. In February 1983, the United Artists was listed on the National Register of Historic Places as part of the Grand Circus Park Historic District. But as time has shown in Detroit, such a designation does not always bring protection. On November 2, 1987, a shower of hundreds of bricks fell from the thirteenth floor of the UA's tower onto Clifford Street, crushing Detroiter Barbara Simons's 1984 Oldsmobile Cutlass Ciera. "At first the police were telling me they couldn't make an accident report because this was an act of God," she told the *Detroit News* at the time.

The seatless balcony offers standing room-only views of the crumbling opulence. The UA was built exclusively for films—a rarity at the time.

Opposite: The outer lobby features these multistory maidens that greeted generations of moviegoers. Only two of the original six are intact.

While no one was injured, it was at least the second time a car had been destroyed by bricks falling off the UA. Kevin Moloney of Detroit said that his 1972 Oldsmobile Cutlass Supreme was hit in the same spot in August 1984.

The UA hit the auction block in New York on September 22, 1989, fetching a mere $460,000; it was expected to go for up to $1 million. The winning bidder was New York investor David Grossman, who bought the United Artists complex with the intent of restoring it and developing the office tower into lofts. His plans were never fully realized.

On October 27, 1995, Mayor Dennis Archer and Detroit Tigers owner Mike Ilitch announced that a new baseball stadium would be built on twenty-five acres on the west side of Grand Circus Park, knocking out a significant number of buildings, including the UA. Businessman and cable television tycoon Don Barden secured a development option on the UA in the mid-1990s and bought the building in January 1997, planning on using either the building or the site for one of the city's three casinos that had been approved by voters. Some in the casino industry said that the property was too small and couldn't be developed into a Las Vegas–style gaming hall. Barden was soon approached by city officials, who said they wanted the property for the baseball stadium project. Barden gave them an option to buy the property, and the city transferred that option to Ilitch's Olympia Development in mid-March.

Such beauty among such destruction. The sights of the movie palaces themselves were considered almost as important as what was on the screen.

Barden later lost out on his bid to land one of the casino licenses. A spokeswoman for Olympia Development told the *Free Press* in late March 1997 that Ilitch planned to tear down the theatre, the building, or both, and use the site for parking. Ilitch has bought many historic structures surrounding Comerica Park and the theatre district and done just that.

Changing Hands, Unchanging Condition

Today, the theatre still stands, and Ilitch's companies have not made public any plans to redevelop the property. Perhaps because he planned to have the building meet the wrecking ball, the UA was left to sit and rot, demolished by neglect and at times left wide open to trespass. The interior has been stripped of most of its décor and has been exposed to the elements. The Detroit City Council ordered the building to be demolished in 2001, but an Ilitch lawyer asked for a reprieve, saying it would be refurbished. In May 2003, the building went back on the city's hit list.

"Our history in the City of Detroit is one of restoration," an Olympia spokesman told the *Free Press* in 2004. "However, it is not possible to save every building in the city because it's not economically feasible for every structure." Ilitch has a fortune of about $1.5 billion and is in the top 250 wealthiest people in the country, according to *Forbes* magazine. His family owns or controls more than 150 properties in downtown Detroit.

Starting in the late 1990s, the building's windows became a blank canvas for the region's graffiti artists. Hundreds of the UA's windows were filled with artwork, including many inspired by Mayan hieroglyphics in gold, reds and blues. The *Free Press* even backed the illegal art project in an editorial in August 2004, writing that the graffiti shows "how enlivening art can spring from a blighted canvas" and that "even those who don't like urban art would be hard pressed to argue that it makes the façade of a rotting building any worse." Still, critics and many metro Detroiters deemed it nothing but vandalism.

In December 2005, with Detroit's Super Bowl fast approaching, Ilitch cleaned up the building, possibly to avoid negative media attention. The UA's rusty marquee was dismantled, and the graffiti was removed from every window. The *Free Press* decried the scrub-down in an editorial that December as "a misguided attempt to clean up for the Super Bowl, as if the urban art is more offensive than the empty building," and added, "Out-of-towners would have found it fascinating, the kind of cool government planners can't possibly manufacture." Kevin Joy, one of the main artists behind the art in the windows, asked the *Free Press* in August 2006: "What's more preposterous: a giant Mayan temple in Detroit or spending money to have it all removed and let it continue to sit empty?"

This view of the theatre's auditorium gives an overview of the damage that it has sustained at the hands of a leaky roof, negligent owners, vandals and scrappers.

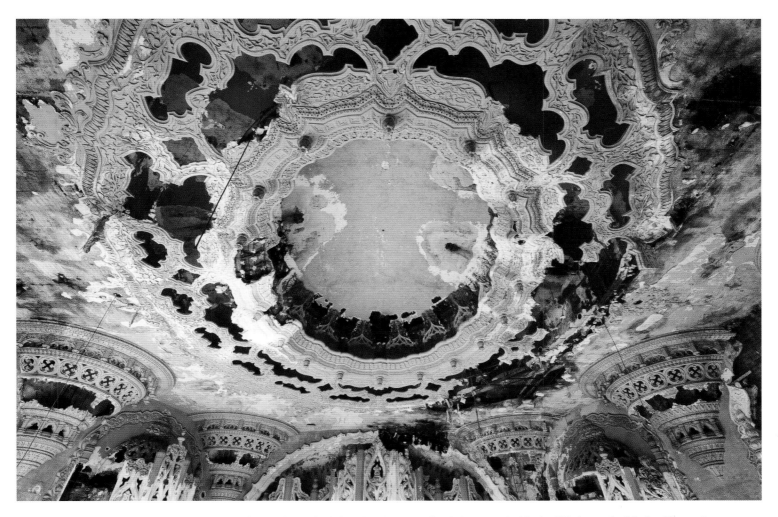

The ceiling, badly destroyed by water damage, hints at the majestic interior that once dazzled patrons inside the "Shrine to the Motion Picture."

Since 2005, the UA also has received new doors and a new roof, and a yellow debris chute dangles from the top floor. Video surveillance cameras have been mounted near the building's entrances, and a fence was erected around its perimeter in late 2006. The building is significantly cleaner and more secure, but the screen is still dark and the building still vacant, just as it has been for thirty-seven of its eighty-two years.

The ceiling bowls are mostly intact, though they haven't been spared destruction at the hands of scrappers. The theatre was allowed to sit and rot for years, perhaps because it is believed its owner planned to tear it down.

THE VANITY BALLROOM

Couples used to swing to big band sounds and rock out to The MC5 and The Stooges in an Aztec temple on the city's east side.

The Vanity Ballroom opened on October 28, 1929, the eve of the stock market crash. It followed several other dance venues that opened in the 1920s, but because of the Great Depression, it was the last ballroom to open in the city. Despite the Depression, the Vanity was one of the most popular dance venues in town and a place generations of Detroiters went to hear live performances by Duke Ellington, Benny Goodman, Louis Prima, Count Basie, Jimmy and Tommy Dorsey and Cab Calloway. Those who didn't make it out to the Vanity could often tune in their radios for broadcasts from the ballroom.

Such spectacular venues were popular places for Detroiters to dance the night away and socialize. In its heyday, the Vanity hosted huge crowds, often up to one thousand couples. Five nights a week, they danced to the big bands on the fifty-six-hundred-square-foot maple dance floor, where jitterbugging couples "floated" on springs that gave the floor bounce. Patrons—who paid thirty-five cents to get in—would enter from Newport Street and ascend a grand main staircase before entering a ballroom that took them to a different time and place.

MEET ME AT THE TEMPLE

In designing the Vanity, architect Charles Agree took the Art Deco style and ran with it. Although exotic elements—in this case, from the Aztec—are common in Art Deco, Agree's desire to create a fantasy setting for dancing and entertainment led to a design almost more exotic than Art Deco. The ballroom is filled with

The Vanity Ballroom lights up East Jefferson Avenue in 1930, a year after it opened on the eve of the stock market crash. *Photo from the Detroit Free Press archives.*

The Art Deco exterior still impresses today with its elaborate, colorful brickwork. The Vanity is the last intact ballroom of Detroit's great dance halls of the big band era.

stepped archways, rich earth-toned colors and Aztec symbols, all inspired by pre-Columbian archaeological discoveries of the time. Stylized Indian heads, stepped-brick archways and green glazed tiles hovered over the dancers' heads. Chandelier medallions clung to the ceiling. Ornate Aztec-styled sconces lit darkened corners. Tiny tables with miniature lamps huddled on the outskirts of the dance floor.

The dance floor had two long bars, an enormous cloakroom, a bandstand, a soda fountain and a revolving chandelier with light-reflecting mirrors. The Vanity did not sell alcohol, instead offering ginger ale and juices for a dime. Everything from the light fixtures to the curtain behind the stage had an Aztec- or Mayan-inspired design. The latter featured a scene of the temples at Chichen Itza. A huge blade sign, spelling out "Vanity" in bold vertical letters and "dancing" horizontally below it, hung over the East Jefferson Avenue side and let Detroiters know where the action was.

The Vanity was built and run by Edward J. Strata for thirty years. He and his business partner, Edward J. Davis, had built the Grande Ballroom across town on the west side in 1928. The ballrooms, including the price of land, cost the men about $500,000 (about $6.2 million today, when adjusted for inflation). The Vanity is, for all intents and purposes, the sister of the Grande. The Vanity catered to the city's east side and eastern suburbs; the Grande lured those on the west. Both were designed by Agree, and, like the Grande, the Vanity's

ballroom is on the second floor. Facing Jefferson are five shop spaces. At one time, there was a Cunningham's drugstore on the corner, with Friedberger's jewelry store, a Harry Suffrin's men's clothing store, Burns Shoes and other familiar names in the remaining spaces. There also was an ice cream shop for those date nights when couples wanted to share a milkshake before a night of dancing.

During the 1930s and early '40s, the ballroom held theme nights. Wednesdays and Thursdays were "stag nights." On Sundays, up to nine hundred couples would jam the floor and dance to the Woody Herman Orchestra, Tony Pastor or Claude Thornhill.

Theresa Binno was no stranger to the city's dance halls during the 1940s, frequenting the Graystone and Grande ballrooms, as well as the Vanity. When she was eighteen or nineteen years old, her father would drop her and her girlfriends off for either a date or a night of swing or swaying to "Moonlight Serenade" or "Begin the Beguine."

"It was just dancing, no liquor or any of that," said Binno, now eighty and living in Waterford, Michigan. "We'd go in the early evening and spend three or four hours dancing, drinking Cokes…Someone would always ask us to dance. We were always dancing.

"I said I'd never get married unless the guy knew how to dance…It was a great time to be young," added Binno, who hasn't seen the Vanity in about fifty years. "Everyone there knew how to dance. Nowadays, it seems like no one knows how to dance."

The colorful brickwork and a pair of the hieroglyphs that dot the Vanity's exterior. Duke Ellington, Benny Goodman, Count Basie and Cab Calloway were among those who performed here.

By the 1950s, times had changed. Televisions were in many households, and rock was in and ballroom dancing was out. Bingo nights were often the only thing paying the bills.

"In the 1940s and early '50s the cost of musicians started going up so that the era of the big bands was over," Strata, then seventy-five, told the *Detroit Free Press* in 1964. "And, too, the taste of young people has changed so drastically that they just want rock 'n' roll and won't support a big ballroom anymore." With the decline of big bands, the Vanity ran into problems and closed in 1958. It would later reopen in February 1964, opening once a week or so, mainly catering to older people looking to relive the swing era. Admission was $1.25.

While Strata still owned the building, the dances were run by the city's Department of Parks and Recreation as part of then-Mayor Jerome Cavanagh's Departmental Council on Aging. In addition to the occasional dance, the Vanity housed church and civic club events. The attendance was modest. The city had hoped for 250 tickets to be sold to the dances, but barely half that would show.

Strata died the following year, and LeRoy B. McAnally—who was the legal guardian for Strata's widow—tried his hand at running the Vanity for a few years. While McAnally had danced at the Vanity in his younger years, he had little desire for the business, keeping it open, "frankly, because we felt it would help sell the building," he told the *Detroit Free Press* in June 1975.

It so happened that ballroom dancing enjoyed a renewed interest in the mid-1970s, mostly among middle-aged folks who used to dance in their youths. "You can only read so much, you can only watch the boob tube so much, then you have to do something to relieve the boredom," Sam Leeds told the *Free Press* in 1975. He and his wife, Helen, were among those who came to relive their youth by dancing under the red and blue lights on the Vanity's dance floor.

While the crowds paled in comparison to its glory days, the Vanity joined YMCAs and other venues in offering occasional dances. But if the decline in dancing wasn't enough of a challenge, the neighborhood around the Vanity started going downhill fast around the same time. Guards had to walk visitors to their cars—a surefire turnoff for business.

The building was sold to the Van Mineff Corp., a small group of investors, in 1971. It was in this incarnation that it would play host to Detroit rock acts such as The MC5, The Stooges, Ted Nugent and The Amboy Dukes and others that also frequented the Grande. "I can only imagine the effect on some kid's acid trip forty years ago at some rock show when all those pre-Columbian faces started becoming animated," said John Carlisle, who writes the popular "DetroitBlog." "What a great backdrop for a psychedelic experience. What a strange setting for a concert." Yet much like its sister, the Grande (which closed in late 1972), the Vanity could not survive the decline of garage rock or the decline of Detroit following the 1967 riot. The deterioration of the Jefferson-Chalmers area knocked out all of the storefronts' tenants in the 1970s.

The Aztec ballroom now resembles an Aztec ruin, with gaping holes in the ceiling and a collapsed wall along the stage. Ballrooms like the Vanity were popular places for Detroiters to dance the night away.

Faces carved into the ballroom's arches watch over the Vanity, helpless to stop the elements, scavengers or time.

SAVE THE LAST DANCE

In 1980, twin brothers Ronald and Donald Murphy bought the Vanity from Van Mineff for $200,000. The twins were tour guides at Greenfield Village, a museum in nearby Dearborn, and loved history and classic architecture. The Murphys and James Demick had a mutual interest in "gluing Detroit back together," the *Free Press* wrote in January 1980, and found their chance when they snuck into the abandoned Vanity through a wide-open door. What they saw shocked them. Amidst busted windows and battered concrete, vagrants had taken roost, and the dance floor once filled with dancing couples was now littered with broken bottles and trash. A failing roof had damaged the floating dance floor.

"I just thought it was so beautiful. It was just a shambles," Demick told the *Detroit News* in 1980. "The city was planning to tear it down, but we wanted to save it."

The brothers set off on one of the more ambitious restoration projects in the city's history. They found that Agree was still alive, then eighty-two and living

Many of the Vanity's plaster details are in remarkable shape, like an ancient Aztec tomb on the east side. The ballroom was added to the National Register of Historic Places in 1982.

in Southfield, a nearby suburb of Detroit. They contacted him and consulted photos to "make sure the restored Vanity Ballroom is just like the original." They got to work puttying and mopping the place back into shape. They envisioned jazz, disco, parties and even a return to ballroom dancing.

The Claude Neon Tubelite marquee hadn't worked for years. The five storefronts were vacant. But the ballroom floor and its booths were in surprisingly good shape considering the landmark had been wide-open for several years before the Murphys bought it. The floor was in reasonable shape but suffering from water damage from a leaky roof. The plaster hieroglyphs had survived, as had the mural decorating the stage wall. They repainted with the same rich china blue used when the building opened fifty years earlier and wired a 1936 Wurlitzer jukebox into the overhead speakers. They started off small, renting it out for everything from discos to fraternal conventions and had a formal "grand opening" on October 4, 1980, with Woody Herman and His New Thundering Herd headlining.

The Vanity would be the city's last great rock venue, having outlived the Eastown and Riviera Theatres, the Grande and the Michigan Palace. But the Vanity faced the challenges of a shrinking city and a location far from downtown and was fighting a decaying neighborhood. The lack of a liquor license didn't help, either. The twins and Demick folded. The ballroom would have brief periods of renewed life, but they were never long-lasting.

As testament to the Vanity's architectural and cultural importance, the ballroom was listed on the National Register of Historic Places on November 12, 1982.

Today, a feeling reminiscent of the *Indiana Jones* movies overwhelms you as you ascend from the entry stairs into the Aztec ruins of the ballroom. The Vanity is hurting yet salvageable. It remains the last intact ballroom of Detroit's great dance halls of the big band era of the early 1930s and late 1940s. It has largely been spared the ravages of scrappers and vandals, though its walls have crumbled in places, there is water damage in spots and some of its paint has lost its luster. Its towering outdoor marquee, which had become rusted and worn, was removed in the early 1990s. Some of its architectural details were chiseled off and stolen. Its massive coat-check room is filled with nothing but empty hooks. Its dance floor is mostly intact, other than some buckled floorboards and the noticeable lack of any jitterbugging couples.

Woodward Avenue Presbyterian Church

In the middle of the city limits sits Woodward Avenue Presbyterian Church, arguably Detroit's most gorgeous church, silently awaiting a resurrection.

As Detroit continued to grow, it was decided that a church was needed to serve what was then the city's northern reaches. The congregation gathered for its first meeting of worship at the Christian Church on November 3, 1907. The Reverend J.M. Barkley preached from 1 Chronicles 28:10: "Take heed now for the Lord has chosen you to build a house for the sanctuary; be strong and do it." And get started on doing it, the congregation did.

Meetings were held within the week, discussing everything from articles of association to raising money to what to name their future home: Northminster, Duffield, Church of the Redeemer, Monteith, John Knox or Woodward Avenue. On December 10 of that year, the civil organization of the church was completed, and the congregation voted to be named the Woodward Avenue Presbyterian Church. The congregation petitioned the Presbytery of Detroit on February 14, 1908, to organize the church and was given the go-ahead, gaining official admittance on March 17, 1908.

The Reverend Sherman L. Divine was called by unanimous vote to be its first minister and was installed on November 5, 1908. "His optimism, aggressiveness and tremendous energy infused the congregation with a fine spirit of alertness and courage," the church's fiftieth anniversary program said in 1958. It was under Divine's leadership that the church would realize the building of a majestic home of its own. And his plans were grandiose. He envisioned a sanctuary that would cost about $100,000 (about $2.35 million today, when adjusted for inflation). "No infant church in the city and scarcely one throughout the land had ever possessed the faith, and we might say

The English Gothic masterpiece still looks as stately as ever standing along Woodward Avenue. It was added to the National Register of Historic Places in 1982.

Opposite: The Woodward Avenue Presbyterian Church, with its rough rock and limestone façade, shortly after being built in 1911. *Photo from the Burton Historical Collection, Detroit Public Library.*

the audacity, to attempt such a monumental task," the anniversary program said. "There were no rich men behind the enterprise, but there were plenty of young and optimistic followers of the Master ready to put themselves at His disposal for carrying out His purposes."

In September 1908, Tracy and Katherine McGregor donated the property for the church. Katherine McGregor was the daughter of lumber baron David Whitney, whose mansion still stands on Woodward Avenue. She and her husband also donated the church organ and land north of the building for parking and a playground.

The Cleveland-based architectural firm of Badgley and Nicklas designed the building. Sidney Rose Badgley, a prominent church architect at the turn of the century, designed the church in a modern English Gothic style. The cornerstone was cemented into place at a ceremony at 2:30 p.m. January 1, 1910, with coins, copies of the Bible, the constitution of the Presbyterian Church of the USA, a copy of the church manual, the prospectus of the new building, a program from the cornerstone-laying ceremony and copies of the *Northminster Tidings*, *Michigan Presbyterian* and the *Detroit Free Press* of December 31, 1909, sealed inside. Work proceeded quickly, and excitement grew as the congregation continued to sign up new members. The church was dedicated on June 25, 1911, though by that January, trustees had started meeting inside the building and people were admitted into the congregation. At the end of that year, the church on Woodward reported having 742 members.

The church's rough, dark Pennsylvania brownstone was quarried in Polk County and was trimmed in light-colored limestone. The building's most distinguishing feature is a tall, octagonal lantern that rises from the center of the roof and is flanked by twin, low towers that frame the church's gabled entrance. The lantern dome–crowned church is Badgley's calling card, and the Woodward Avenue church is among his finest works and a unique landmark.

"This splendid building…stands as one of the most handsomest churches in the country," the *Detroit Times* wrote on June 10, 1911. Inside, the church is more or less what is known as the Akron Plan style, where an auditorium worship space is surrounded by connecting offices and classrooms for Sunday school. The plan improved efficiency and provided unobstructed views thanks to its vast openness. The sanctuary is filled with dark oak and walnut woodwork and pews and cream-colored walls. The walls in the choir and sanctuary areas are sparingly painted to resemble Byzantine mosaics. Churchgoers would sit before the pulpit in a semicircle with a dramatic, curved wooden balcony above. Eight large chandeliers hang from the octagonal, skylight-lit ceiling above. Windows on all eight sides bathe the sanctuary in natural light.

Divine left the church to become a pastor in Helena, Montana, in 1913, but under his leadership, the church had grown to 1,325 members. Ten years later, in 1921, the church had 2,204 members, making it one of the largest

The sanctuary's rows of wooden pews, stained-glass windows and chandeliers remain—a ghostly house of the holy. The building has suffered significant water damage and will take millions to restore.

Presbyterian congregations in the city of Detroit. In July 1940, the church's nearly 2,000 members unanimously approved the Reverend Herbert Beecher Hudnut as pastor of the church. He was installed on October 18, 1940, and was the longest-serving pastor in the church's history. Throughout more than two decades of leadership, he would preside over some of the biggest changes in the building's history.

Woodward Avenue's "congregation was what I'd call upper middle class," said the Reverend Roy Peterson, a retired Presbyterian minister who served in metro Detroit for nearly three decades starting in the mid-1950s. "Management, professionals, people like that." Wilber Brucker, a governor of Michigan from 1931 to 1932 and U.S. secretary of the army from 1955 to 1961, was a member of Woodward Avenue.

"You had the feeling of belonging to something important going to church there," said Wilma Dellinger, now eighty-nine and living in Troy, Michigan. "It seemed to permeate the place. To go into the church, you knew you were going to someplace special."

Her father, Willis Harvey, was a deacon at the church, and she was baptized there. For almost twenty years, her family attended the church, occasionally taking the streetcars or buses to get there. She and many of the other younger churchgoers usually sat in the swooping, curved balcony.

As the church's upper-middle-class families left Detroit for the suburbs and the city's outskirts,

concerns started to arise about whether it would be able to stay afloat. The church bought land on West 12 Mile Road and Bermuda Lane to serve its relocated members. Services began in the gymnasium of the Northbrook School on September 29, 1957. Hudnut's plan was to leave Woodward Avenue and relocate the 1,250-member congregation to Southfield, a fast-growing northern suburb at the time. The church was eventually built in nearby Beverly Hills instead.

Woodward Avenue put out a book with a lengthy history of its congregation for its fiftieth anniversary in 1958. In it, church elder emeritus William O. Stoddard wrote, "The future of our great church is in the hands of God, as its past has been." Speaking of the expansion in Southfield, he wrote that the church's "history shows that ours has always been a closely-knit, hard-working church. For the present, God has given us a double task, but also, He has given us two hands. Let us use both."

"Herb had big plans," said Peterson, who was at Northbrook from 1964 until 1978 and now lives in Harrisville, Michigan. "But it soon became obvious that it wasn't going to be possible." About 1960, the congregation made it clear that it did not want to leave Detroit. Church members "didn't like the idea, and the congregation voted not to do that. So Northbrook became its own church."

Starting in the 1950s, many whites started leaving for the city's outlying areas or the suburbs—a trend that increased following the city's 1967 riot. These ex-

The marvelous winding, curved balcony is one of the building's most prominent features. Starting in the 1950s, many whites started leaving for the city's outlying areas or the suburbs, founding new churches in their new homes.

The view from the balcony shows that not even a house of God can be spared the ravages of nature and scrappers. At right, note that some of the large organ pipes have been stolen.

Detroiters founded new churches in their new homes, something Peterson refers to as "colonizing in the suburbs." Woodward Avenue Presbyterian started to struggle with less money and lower membership. In 1951, the church had 1,552 members. By 1961, it had 950; and by 1971, its congregation had dwindled to only 404. More than 8,500 people had been members of the church since it opened.

As the city became more racially integrated, the congregation's composition changed with it. Hudnut led "very traditional Presbyterian services for that time," Peterson said. "His style would not have attracted black Presbyterians, so there was no way that church could survive as a neighborhood church…The only churches that survived were those who relocated or had substantial endowments." Hudnut left Woodward Avenue Presbyterian in 1965.

THE MERGER

The Woodward Avenue church's struggles with declining membership were not unique in the city. In a city whose population had declined from nearly 2 million in the early 1950s to 1.2 million in 1980, many churches found that their needs were more than their human and financial resources could muster. Another church in a similar position was the Presbyterian Church of the Covenant across town, on the city's east side.

The Church of the Covenant celebrated its first communion on February 21, 1875, and opened a building on East Grand Boulevard at Preston in January 1908. Its pastor was the Reverend Gary M. Douglas Jr., a former truck driver who once studied law enforcement with the FBI. In March 1981, the Covenant Church's annual report noted that the building needed more than $100,000 worth of repairs, which its members could not afford. The Covenant's congregation voted unanimously to merge with the Woodward Avenue Presbyterian Church. It was a move Peterson calls "a merger of two dying swans."

On June 14, 1981, the remnants of the two congregations met in the sanctuary of the Woodward Avenue church and passed a resolution to merge. On July 19, 1981, both congregations adopted the bylaws of the newly combined church, and the presbytery selected Douglas as the first black minister at the Woodward church. "Another year has come and gone, one which was most trying for all of us," Douglas wrote in the pastor's report for 1981. "One which will go down in history, and will be remembered for years. The uniting of Woodward/Covenant was an act of God in history. Now that we are together, let us move forward in the building of God's kingdom."

Still, even with the merger, the new church reported only 485 members at the end of 1981. By 1985, it had only 247 members filling its giant sanctuary. In 1991, the last year it reported membership to the presbytery, it had 210. While the congregation had dwindled, the

Stained-glass windows in the lantern still fill the church with colorful light, even if it's no longer filled with worshippers.

cost of running the church had not. Douglas proved to be a controversial figure, both in his own congregation and in the Presbyterian Church. He had been a Baptist who converted to Presbyterianism. "Gary had ideas that weren't very Presbyterian," said Dorothy Seabrooks, eighty, an elder at St. John's Presbyterian Church of Detroit who had been in the Woodward Avenue church several times. "He was a maverick."

The Reverend Ed Gehris was the executive presbyter in Detroit from 1987 to 1999 and was in charge when Woodward Avenue Presbyterian changed hands, leaving the presbytery for good. The presbytery "had tried working with him for five of six years," investing $85,000 to $90,000 for a new heating system for the church because the congregation couldn't come up with the cash on its own, Gehris said.

The presbytery fought hard to keep Woodward Avenue Presbyterian open, Gehris said, because it was one of only two Presbyterian congregations left on Woodward Avenue, the city's main drag. "We'd closed churches and closed churches, and there was a strong feeling we should support them and keep them open," said Gehris, who is now retired and living near Philadelphia. "The presbytery did just about everything it could to make that church survive." But there was only so much the presbytery could do. The building was in tremendous disrepair. The congregation couldn't afford to pay Douglas's salary, let alone maintain a building of that size. Worse, Douglas wanted to split from the Presbyterian Church and take Woodward Avenue in a different direction. The presbytery "had a pastor that they were unhappy with," added Peterson, "and he was unhappy with the presbytery. So it is my impression they let him buy the church to get rid of him."

Last Rites

In the spring of 1993, the matter of breaking from the Presbyterian Church was put up for a vote before the congregation. Perhaps because even those who didn't support Douglas wanted to see the struggling church survive, the move passed. A May 27, 1993 letter to the Woodward Avenue congregation alerted them that the church was being turned over to Douglas on a quitclaim deed. The letter said that a four-party agreement had been reached the day before between Woodward Avenue Presbyterian, Douglas, the Presbytery of Detroit and the Woodward Avenue Protestant Church of Christ (the name the building would go by after changing hands).

Under the agreement, Douglas renounced the jurisdiction of the Presbyterian Church and was no longer a Presbyterian minister. Because of the merger between Woodward Avenue and the Church of the Covenant twelve years earlier, the deal marked the end of two longtime Presbyterian congregations in Detroit. Douglas was left with only those he'd brought in, and a small congregation got smaller. The church "really was in

Looking toward the heavens from the church's sanctuary. In 1921, the church had 2,204 members and was one of the largest Presbyterian congregations in the city. By 1985, it had only 247.

Magnificent painting and plasterwork adorn the walls above the church's stained-glass windows. In 1993, the church voted to leave the Presbyterian Church, sealing its fate.

disrepair when the Presbytery gave it to Gary," Seabrooks said. "Everything was going wrong in there."

Douglas eventually took the building in a different direction, and it became the Abyssinia Interdenominational Church, a Baptist church that traces its roots to Ethiopia. The building limped along until Douglas's death in January 2004 and then became locked in court battles among Douglas's estate, the church and his widow. In the meantime, holes in the roof let in the elements, which started eating away at its wooden floors and the plaster in the sanctuary. The building also became a victim of theft and vandalism, and its organ pipes were scrapped in the fall of 2009.

In November 2009, the Cathedral of Praise Baptist Church acquired the building and planned to renovate it. Its pastor, Kenneth Brock, said he planned to restore the sanctuary to its original splendor and have its first service in July 2010. As of October 2010, the church remained empty, in disrepair and far from a second life. "We have a vision for this building, and the lord has given us a vision for this building and this neighborhood," Brock said. Being able to pay for what will surely be a multimillion-dollar project, he continued, "is going to be by faith."

Peterson lamented, "It grieves me to see, not just Woodward Avenue, but to see all these churches that have declined. It's heartbreaking. But Presbyterians here have been known to be worshippers of their God, not their buildings."

SPECIAL THANKS

William M. Worden, John Gallagher, Janel Yamashiro, John Cassidy, Deborah Austin, Paul and Ann Austin, Stephen Austin, the *Detroit Free Press*, the Burton Historical Collection, the Manning Brothers Collection, Michael Hauser, John Lauter, Roger Lesinski, Rebecca Binno Savage, Kari Smith, Joel Stone, Karen Nagher, Joe Gartrell, Lucas McGrail, the readers of BuildingsofDetroit.com and HistoricDetroit.org, all of those who shared their stories with us, Amy and Michael Doerr, Robert Klatt, Dan and Silke Seybold, Maya Fardoun, Andrew Moore, David Paris, Yves Marchand, Romain Meffre, Richard Ayers and Norma Martínez.

ABOUT THE AUTHOR

AUTHOR DAN AUSTIN is a journalist and Detroit historian. Having worked at newspapers across the country, he returned to his beloved Motor City in 2006 and tells the stories behind the city's forgotten landmarks at HistoricDetroit.org.

ABOUT THE PHOTOGRAPHER

PHOTOGRAPHER SEAN DOERR has been documenting abandoned and neglected architecture around metro Detroit since the age of fourteen. In addition to being published in many publications, his work can be seen at www.snweb.org.